I R I S H

EMIGRATION LISTS

1833 – 1839

IRISH
EMIGRATION LISTS
1833 – 1839

Lists of Emigrants Extracted from the
Ordnance Survey Memoirs for
Counties Londonderry and Antrim

Compiled Under the Direction of
BRIAN MITCHELL

CLEARFIELD

Reprinted for
Clearfield Company, Inc. by
Genealogical Publishing Co., Inc.
Baltimore, Maryland
2003

INTRODUCTION

T he Ordnance Survey was founded in 1791 owing to the threat of an invasion from France during the Napoleonic Wars. The military need for an accurate map of southern England, at the scale of 1" to 1 mile, resulted in the first sheet, covering part of Kent, appearing in 1801.

With the end of the war in 1815 the practical value of maps based on very exact measurement, within a framework of control points known as triangulation stations, was widely appreciated, and this resulted in the survey being extended to cover the whole of Britain.

In Ireland, as a prelude to a nationwide valuation of land and buildings (the so-called Griffiths Valuation), the Ordnance Survey was directed to map the whole country at a scale of 6" to 1 mile. The resultant 6" maps, in effect a record of Ireland's 60,462 townlands, appeared between 1835 and 1846. In the Griffiths Valuation, carried out between 1848 and 1864, every townland was identified against the appropriate Ordnance Survey sheet number.

It was originally intended to accompany each map with written topographical descriptions, or memoirs, for every civil parish. But only one memoir, for the Parish of Templemore, County Londonderry, had been published when the idea was abandoned in 1840. It was planned that the memoir for each parish should be no more than six pages. Templemore Parish, which included the city of Londonderry, needed 350 pages; and the cost of £1,700 in producing it was three times more than the original budget for the whole county. Furthermore, the publication of Samuel Lewis' two-volume *Topographical Dictionary of Ireland* in 1837 weakened the case for the memoirs.

The field officers did, however, gather much historical, geographical, economic and social information for many parishes in their notebooks. The original notes and manuscripts can now be found in fifty-two boxes in the Royal Irish Academy in Dublin. They cover nineteen of Ireland's counties. Counties Antrim and Londonderry contain by far the most detailed information, with seventeen and twenty boxes, respectively, of work papers. Counties Donegal, Down, Fermanagh and Tyrone consist of two or three boxes, whereas the remainder, Counties Armagh, Cavan, Cork, Galway,

Leitrim, Leix, Longford, Mayo, Meath, Monaghan, Roscommon, Sligo and Tipperary, have only one or part of one box each.

The memoirs for Counties Antrim and Londonderry are unique in that for many of their parishes lists of emigrants for a few years in the mid to late 1830s were compiled. As emigration records these lists are unparalleled. At the American end the so-called customs passenger lists, which record the arrival of all immigrants from 1820, provide only two clues relating to the origin of the emigrants—the port of departure of the ship and the nationality of the passenger. As a means of identifying the Irish homeland of an ancestor these lists have limitations. By contrast, the lists in the Ordnance Survey memoirs identify both the destination of the emigrant and his place of origin in Ireland—the primary objective of any American tracing his Irish ancestry. In addition, the age, townland address, year of emigration, and religious denomination are given for each emigrant named in the memoir. The usefulness of this information is self-evident. With an age and a religious denomination, for example, it should be possible to identify the baptism entry of an ancestor.

Besides the names of ordinary emigrants from Antrim and Londonderry, the names of seasonal migrants to the harvests in England and Scotland are included in this book, as in many cases seasonal migration acted as a prelude to emigration rather than an alternative to it. The cheapness of travel between Ireland and Britain and between Britain and America encouraged "step-wise" migration. An emigrant could walk to a seaport such as Londonderry, pay one shilling to cross the Irish Sea, save a few pounds from harvest work in the Glasgow and Liverpool areas and, finally, buy a transatlantic passage. These seasonal migrants, where recorded in the memoirs, are listed in this work on separate pages.

Acknowledgements

Many thanks to Robert Wright and Ciaran Doherty who extracted the names of the immigrants from microfilm copies of the memoirs supplied by the Royal Irish Academy, Dublin. Michael McLaughlin and Eamonn Doherty checked through the transcribed work sheets. The index was created on computer by Norman Surko and Eamon Burke. The lists and index were typed by Roisin Bonar. All are on the staff of the North West Centre for Learning and Development, Londonderry. Funding of the project was made possible by the Northern Ireland Department of Economic Development.

Brian Mitchell

Key To Religious Denominations

RC	ROMAN CATHOLIC
EC	ESTABLISHED CHURCH
P	PRESBYTERIAN
S	SECEDER
I	INDEPENDENT
M	METHODIST
MO	MORAVIAN
COV	COVENANTER
BAP	BAPTIST

THE PARISHES OF COUNTY ANTRIM

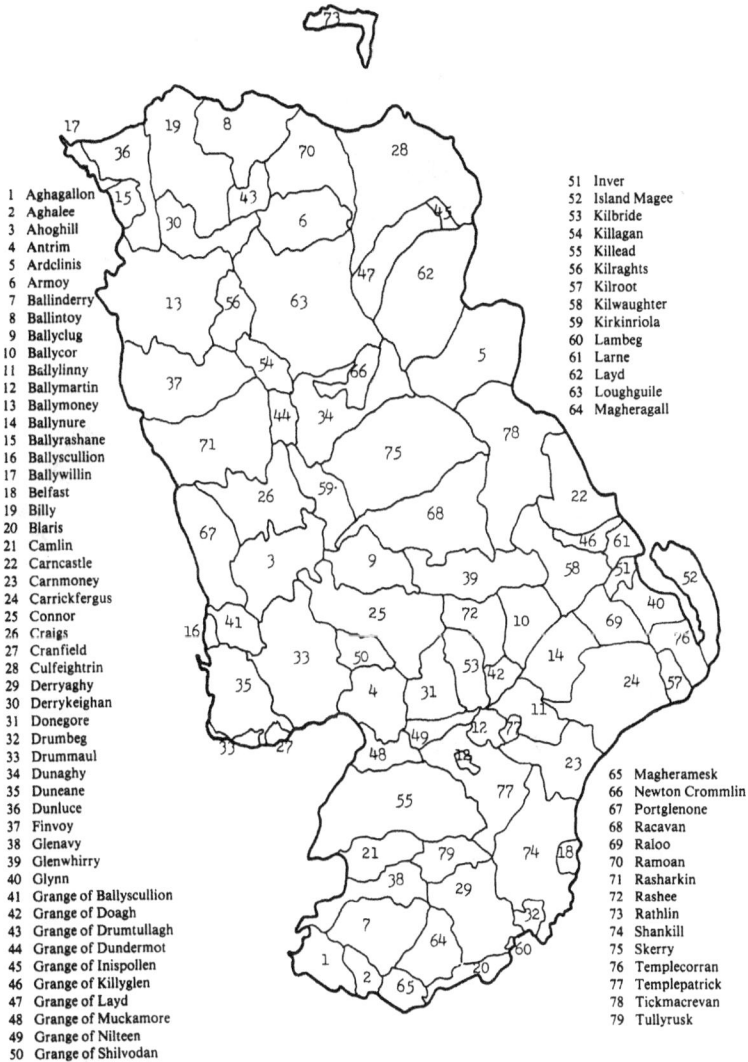

1 Aghagallon
2 Aghalee
3 Ahoghill
4 Antrim
5 Ardclinis
6 Armoy
7 Ballinderry
8 Ballintoy
9 Ballyclug
10 Ballycor
11 Ballylinny
12 Ballymartin
13 Ballymoney
14 Ballynure
15 Ballyrashane
16 Ballyscullion
17 Ballywillin
18 Belfast
19 Billy
20 Blaris
21 Camlin
22 Carncastle
23 Carnmoney
24 Carrickfergus
25 Connor
26 Craigs
27 Cranfield
28 Culfeightrin
29 Derryaghy
30 Derrykeighan
31 Donegore
32 Drumbeg
33 Drummaul
34 Dunaghy
35 Duneane
36 Dunluce
37 Finvoy
38 Glenavy
39 Glenwhirry
40 Glynn
41 Grange of Ballyscullion
42 Grange of Doagh
43 Grange of Drumtullagh
44 Grange of Dundermot
45 Grange of Inispollen
46 Grange of Killyglen
47 Grange of Layd
48 Grange of Muckamore
49 Grange of Nilteen
50 Grange of Shilvodan

51 Inver
52 Island Magee
53 Kilbride
54 Killagan
55 Killead
56 Kilraghts
57 Kilroot
58 Kilwaughter
59 Kirkinriola
60 Lambeg
61 Larne
62 Layd
63 Loughguile
64 Magheragall

65 Magheramesk
66 Newton Crommlin
67 Portglenone
68 Racavan
69 Raloo
70 Ramoan
71 Rasharkin
72 Rashee
73 Rathlin
74 Shankill
75 Skerry
76 Templecorran
77 Templepatrick
78 Tickmacrevan
79 Tullyrusk

THE PARISHES OF COUNTY LONDONDERRY

1 Aghadowey	
2 Aghanloo	
3 Agivey	25 Drumachose
4 Arboe	26 Dunboe
5 Artrea	27 Dungiven
6 Ballinderry	28 Errigal
7 Ballyaghran	29 Faughanvale
8 Ballymoney	30 Formoyle
9 Ballynascreen	31 Kilcronaghan
10 Ballyrashane	32 Kildollagh
11 Ballyscullion	33 Killelagh
12 Ballywillin	34 Killowen
13 Balteagh	35 Kilrea
14 Banagher	36 Learmount
15 Bovevagh	37 Lissan
16 Carrick	38 Macosquin
17 Clondermot	39 Maghera
18 Coleraine	40 Magherafelt
19 Cumber Lower	41 Tamlaght
20 Cumber Upper	42 Tamlaght Finlagan
21 Derryloran	43 Tamlaght O'Crilly
22 Desertlyn	44 Tamlaghtard
23 Desertmartin	45 Templemore
24 Desertoghill	46 Termoneeny

COUNTY: ANTRIM
PARISH: AGHAGALLON

NAME	AGE	YEAR LEFT	TOWNLAND	DESTINATION	RELI-GION
GRIBBIN, Patrick	30	1836	Derrynasser	New York	RC
GRIBBIN, Eleanor	29	1836	Derrynasser	New York	RC
GRIBBIN, Patrick	4	1836	Derrynasser	New York	RC
McSTRAVACK, Patrick	24	1836	Derrymore	Quebec	RC
DOONE, Margaret	25	1836	Derrymore	Quebec	RC
KELLY, James	48	1836	Derrymore	Quebec	RC
KELLY, Mary	46	1836	Derrymore	Quebec	RC
NUGENT, Arthur	25	1837	Ballykeel	New York	RC
McDONNALD, Jean	24	1837	Ballykeel	New York	RC
CARVILLE, James	24	1837	Drumaleet	New York	RC
CARVILLE, Eliza	26	1837	Drumaleet	New York	RC
CARVILLE, James	4	1837	Drumaleet	New York	RC
CARVILLE, Eliza	2	1837	Drumaleet	New York	RC
FALOON, Eliza	55	1837	Derrypark	New York	EC
FALOON, William	23	1837	Derrypark	New York	EC
FALOON, Susana	20	1837	Derrypark	New York	EC

COUNTY: ANTRIM
PARISH: AGHALEE

NAME	AGE	YEAR LEFT	TOWNLAND	DESTINATION	RELI-GION
CHAPMAN, George Crooks	24	1835	Aghadrumglashy	New York	EC

COUNTY: ANTRIM

PARISH: AHOGHILL

NAME	AGE	YEAR LEFT	TOWNLAND	DESTINATION	RELI-GION
McKEON, Thomas	44	1835	Galgorm	New York	P
McKEON, James	10	1835	Galgorm	New York	P
McKEON, Jane	8	1835	Galgorm	New York	P
RICHIE, Robert	30	1835	Galgorm	Quebec	P
McFALL, John	30	1835	Galgorm	Quebec	RC
RUDDEN, John	50	1835	Aughnahoy	New York	P
RUDDEN, Margaret	60	1835	Aughnahoy	New York	P
KERNAHAN, Hugh	22	1835	Moyasset	Quebec	P
KERNAHAN, Nancy	20	1835	Moyasset	Quebec	P
KERNAHAN, Jane	1½	1835	Moyasset	Quebec	P
MORAN, William	32	1835	Watercloney	Liverool	RC
McGONAGLE, Esther	40	1835	Cordonaghy	New York	COV
KENNEDY, John	21	1835	Moneydollog	New York	P
KENNEDY, Anne	23	1835	Moneydollog	New York	P
MAGEE, John	26	1835	Straid	Glasgow	RC
McALISTER, Daniel	22	1835	Straid	Glasgow	RC
CROSSET, Martha	30	1835	Garvaghy	St John	S
CROSSET, Jane	10	1835	Garvaghy	St John	S
CROSSET, Elizabeth	8	1835	Garvaghy	St John	S
CROSSET, James	6	1835	Garvaghy	St John	S
WILEY, Robert	26	1835	Garvaghy	New York	P
McKENNY, Daniel	50	1835	Mullinsallagh	Sydney	EC
LOUGHBRIDGE, Robert	18	1835	Cullybackey	Quebec	EC
KENNEDY, John	20	1835	Moneydollog	Quebec	EC
KENNEDY, Anne	22	1835	Moneydollog	Quebec	EC
KEENAN, Michael	35	1835	Carmagrim	Quebec	RC
KEENAN, Sarah	22	1835	Carmagrim	Quebec	RC
KEENAN, Jane	1	1835	Carmagrim	Quebec	RC
McCAHEY, David	25	1835	Killycoogan	Quebec	P
McCAHEY, Eliza	21	1835	Killycoogan	Quebec	P
ARTHBUTNOT, Robert	25	1835	Killycoogan	Quebec	P
KYLE, Anne	30	1835	Killycoogan	Quebec	P
KYLE, James	32	1835	Killycoogan	Quebec	P
KYLE, William	12	1835	Killycoogan	Quebec	P
KYLE, John	10	1835	Killycoogan	Quebec	P
KYLE, Robert	8	1835	Killycoogan	Quebec	P
KYLE, Joseph	6	1835	Killycoogan	Quebec	P
KYLE, Mary Anne	4	1835	Killycoogan	Quebec	P
KYLE, Elizabeth	2	1835	Killycoogan	Quebec	P
MURRAY, John	24	1835	Ballymontenagh	Glasgow	RC
YOUNG, John	25	1835	Ballymontenagh	Philadelphia	P
SHEIL, Margaret	50	1835	Mullinsallagh	Quebec	P
SHEIL, John	20	1835	Mullinsallagh	Quebec	P
SHEIL, Thomas	18	1835	Mullinsallagh	Quebec	P
SHEIL, Margaret Jun	16	1835	Mullinsallagh	Quebec	P
KEENAN, Michael	36	1835	Largy	Quebec	P
KEENAN, Ellen	25	1835	Largy	Quebec	P
KEENAN, Rose	1	1835	Largy	Quebec	P
KEENAN, Mary	3	1835	Largy	Quebec	P
WISEMAN, Archy	20	1835	Ballywatermoy	New York	P
WILEY, Robert	22	1835	Tullaghgarley	New York	P
ADAIR, Mary Anne	22	1836	Brocklamont	New York	P
ADAIR, Ellen Nora	17	1836	Brocklamont	New York	P
RAY, James	40	1836	Galgorm	Philadelphia	MO
RAY, Jane	40	1836	Galgorm	Philadelphia	MO
RAY, Elizabeth	10	1836	Galgorm	Philadelphia	MO
RAY, Sarah	8	1836	Galgorm	Philadelphia	MO
RAY, William John	6	1836	Galgorm	Philadelphia	MO
RAY, James Jun	2	1836	Galgorm	Philadelphia	MO
COLUM, Margaret	23	1836	Galgorm	New York	P
COLUM, Jane	30	1836	Galgorm	New York	P
COLUM, Robert	20	1836	Galgorm	New York	P
TOOLE, Mary Anne	20	1836	Galgorm	New York	RC

COUNTY: ANTRIM
PARISH: AHOGHILL

NAME	AGE	YEAR LEFT	TOWNLAND	DESTINATION	RELI- GION
CONWELL, Eliza	21	1836	Ahoghill	New York	EC
ADAMS, Mary	28	1836	Aughnahoy	New York	P
HAMMIL, Samuel	21	1836	Aughnahoy	New York	P
HAMMIL, Rose	40	1836	Aughnahoy	New York	P
HAMMIL, James	28	1836	Aughnahoy	New York	P
MAXWELL, Alexander	22	1836	Aughnahoy	New York	P
McCLERNON, Frank	24	1836	Watercloney	New York	RC
McCLERNON, James Henry	22	1836	Watercloney	New York	RC
HUNTER, Jane	35	1836	Moneydollog	New York	P
EAGLESON, William	30	1836	Ballyminstra	Quebec	MO
McCAW, James	25	1836	Portglenone	New York	COV
McKINNEY, John	22	1836	Mullinsallagh	Sydney	EC
McKINNEY, Daniel	20	1836	Mullinsallagh	Quebec	EC
McANALLY, James	26	1836	Watercloney	Glasgow	RC
SPENCER, Thomas	20	1836	Tullyaghgarley	New York	P
McCARTNEY, James	42	1836	Gortfad	New York	P
McCARTNEY, Margaret	40	1836	Gortfad	New York	P
McCARTNEY, Archy	19	1836	Gortfad	New York	P
McCARTNEY, William John	17	1836	Gortfad	New York	P
McCARTNEY, Andrew	15	1836	Gortfad	New York	P
McCARTNEY, Thomas	13	1836	Gortfad	New York	P
McCARTNEY, James	11	1836	Gortfad	New York	P
McCARTNEY, Doratha	9	1836	Gortfad	New York	P
McCARTNEY, Alexander	4	1836	Gortfad	New York	P
McCARTNEY, Agness	42	1836	Gortfad	New York	P
McCARTNEY, Archy	23	1836	Gortfad	New York	P
McCARTNEY, Andrew	20	1836	Gortfad	New York	P
McCARTNEY, Joseph	16	1836	Gortfad	New York	P
McCARTNEY, Andrew	25	1836	Gortfad	Glasgow	P
KYLE, Hugh	25	1836	Lisrodden	Quebec	P
KYLE, James	23	1836	Lisrodden	Quebec	P
RAY, James	40	1836	Bracknamuckley	Liverpool	RC
McKENDRY, James	25	1836	Moboy	St John	P
McKENDRY, Peggy Anne	20	1836	Moboy	St John	P
CRAWFORD, James	45	1836	?	St John	P
MEWHINNY, John	19	1836	Castletown	Quebec	EC
McFALLS, John	30	1836	Fenaghy	Philadelphia	RC
MURRAY, James	40	1836	Moneydollog	Glasgow	RC
TOOLE, Mary Anne	21	1836	Cardonaghy	New York	RC
DUFFIN, Catherine	64	1836	Killane	Glasgow	RC
DUFFIN, Margaret	24	1836	Killane	Glasgow	RC
HINDS, Thomas	35	1836	Finkiltagh	New York	P
HINDS, Hesther	37	1836	Finkiltagh	New York	P
HINDS, Eliza	15	1836	Finkiltagh	New York	P
KENNY, James	20	1836	Craigs	St John	P
JOHNSTON, Mary Anne	20	1836	Craigs	St John	COV
GALLOWAY, Robert	20	1836	Craigs	St John	COV
GALLOWAY, James	22	1836	Craigs	St John	COV
MACHONAGHT, William	50	1836	Ballyconnelly	Quebec	P
MACHONAGHT, Elizabeth	50	1836	Ballyconnelly	Quebec	P
MACHONAGHT, James	25	1836	Ballyconnelly	Quebec	P
MACHONAGHT, Alexander	21	1836	Ballyconnelly	Quebec	P
MACHONAGHT, John	15	1836	Ballyconnelly	Quebec	P
MACHONAGHT, William	17	1836	Ballyconnelly	Quebec	P
MACHONAGHT, Eliza	13	1836	Ballyconnelly	Quebec	P
MACHONAGHT, Catherine	11	1836	Ballyconnelly	Quebec	P
SIMPSON, Jane	50	1836	Killyless	St John	P
SIMPSON, William	12	1836	Killyless	St John	P
SIMPSON, Margaret Anne	22	1836	Killyless	St John	P
SIMPSON, James	14	1836	Killyless	St John	P
McKINNEY, James	21	1836	Killyless	St John	P
McCARTNEY, Charles	20	1836	Bracknamuckley	Quebec	P
McCARTNEY, Mary	30	1836	Bracknamuckley	Quebec	P
McCAHEY, David	24	1836	Killycoogan	Quebec	P

COUNTY: ANTRIM

PARISH: AHOGHILL

NAME	AGE	YEAR LEFT	TOWNLAND	DESTINATION	RELI-GION
WISEMAN, Anne	22	1836	Ballywatermoy	New York	P
WILEY, Eliza	25	1836	Tullaghgarley	New York	P
PETERS, James	22	1836	Crankill	Philadelphia	P
WILSON, James	35	1836	Crankill	Philadelphia	P
PETERS, William	30	1836	Crankill	Philadelphia	P
GREGG, James	30	1836	Crankill	Philadelphia	P
MADILL, James	28	1836	Crankill	Philadelphia	P

COUNTY: ANTRIM
PARISH: AHOGHILL

NAME	AGE	YEAR LEFT	TOWNLAND	DESTINATION	RELI- GION
McANALLY, Peter	30		Watercloney	Glasgow	RC
NEESON, Henry	50		Watercloney	Glasgow	RC
NEESON, John	40		Watercloney	Glasgow	RC
HENRY, Catherine	40		Watercloney	Glasgow	RC
MITCHELL, Daniel	30		Carnearney	Glasgow	P
MITCHELL, William	32		Carnearney	Glasgow	P
EWART, Robert	28		Ballyminstra	Glasgow	P
DARRAGH, Patrick	45		Ballyninstra	Glasgow	RC
DARRAGH, James	22		Ballyninstra	Glasgow	RC
DARRAGH, William	16		Ballyninstra	Glasgow	RC
DARRAGH, Eliza	24		Ballyminstra	Glasgow	RC
DAVISON, Ellen	17		Ballymontenagh	Glasgow	P
McKEE, Alexander	21		Ahoghill	Glasgow	P
DEMPSEY, William	21		Ahoghill	Glasgow	P
LOGAN, Daniel	24		Ahoghill	Glasgow	P
MURRAY, Jane	16		Ahoghill	Glasgow	RC
GILLESPIE, Esther	16		Ballymontenagh	Glasgow	P
WITHEROW, Samuel	24		Ballyconnelly	Glasgow	P
BLANEY, Henry	30		Mullinsallagh	Glasgow	RC
WILSON, John	30		Dreen	Glasgow	P
McCLANE, James	40		Dreen	Glasgow	EC
JOHNSTON, Matthew	20		Dreen	Glasgow	COV
GORDON, Edward	23		Dreen	Glasgow	MO
CAULFIELD, Samuel	25		Loan	Glasgow	P
McCRACKEN, William	26		Craigs	Liverpool	EC
BACCUS, Robert	46		Craigs	Liverpool	EC
HENRY, Joseph	50		Craigs	Glasgow	RC
HENRY, John	25		Craigs	Glasgow	RC
HARBESON, Robert	30		Craigs	Glasgow	P
McINTYRE, William	25		Craigs	Glasgow	P
McINTYRE, John	27		Craigs	Glasgow	P
THOMSON, William	25		Craigs	Glasgow	RC
STERLING, Archy	18		Drumrankin	Glasgow	P
MILLAR, James	26		Drumrankin	Glasgow	P
McALEESE, John	18		Drumrankin	Glasgow	P
STERLING, Thomas	18		Drumrankin	Glasgow	P
MALONE, James	25		Drumrankin	Glasgow	P
McCLEERY, James	55		Drumrankin	Glasgow	RC
McMEEHAN, John	38		Drumrankin	Glasgow	P
McCAHERAN, Denis	30		Drumrankin	Glasgow	P
McILVINON, Hugh	24		Loan	Glasgow	P
CAULFIELD, Jane	24		Loan	Glasgow	P
GIBSON, Nancy	35		Loan	Glasgow	P
WINNON, John	30		Loan	Glasgow	P
MILLAR, William John	25		Loan	Glasgow	P
WORKMAN, James	30		Loan	Glasgow	P
DOEY, Robert	26		Loan	Glasgow	P
KELLY, Thomas	26		Craigs	Glasgow	P
MOONEY, Andrew	30		Craigs	Glasgow	P
CLARKE, Hugh	26		Craigs	Glasgow	P
McCLANE, Robert	28		Craigs	Glasgow	P
HOLMES, Hugh	21		Killyless	Glasgow	P
WRIGHT, Joseph	26		Killyless	Glasgow	P
McFALLS, Charles	22		Carmagrim	Liverpool	RC
McFALLS, Dennis	45		Carmagrim	Liverpool	RC
SCULLION, John	48		Carmagrim	Liverpool	RC
BOORMAN, James	38		Carmagrim	Liverpool	RC
McCALISTER, John	28		Gortgole	Glasgow	RC
O'BRYANS, William	26		Gortgole	Glasgow	RC
O'BRYANS, James	24		Gortgole	Glasgow	RC
McATAGGART, John	30		Gortgole	Glasgow	RC
O'HARA, Hamish	26		Bracknamuckley	Glasgow	RC
O'RAW, Patrick	54		Lisnahunshin	Glasgow	RC
GRIBBEN, Neil	40		Lisnahunshin	Glasgow	RC

COUNTY: ANTRIM   SEASONAL MIGRANTS

PARISH: AHOGHILL

NAME	AGE	YEAR LEFT	TOWNLAND	DESTINATION	RELI-GION
O HARA, Henry	30		Lisnahunshin	Glasgow	RC
O'HARA, John	25		Lisnahunshin	Glasgow	RC
WHITELY, Robert	40		Lisnahunshin	Glasgow	COV
BOYDE, Andrew	26		Lisnahunshin	Glasgow	RC
O'HARA, John	22		Lisnahunshin	Glasgow	RC
HENRY, John	30		Lisnahunshin	Glasgow	RC
O'NEILL, Bernard	40		Lisnahunshin	Glasgow	RC
MADDIGAN, Henry	35		Lisnahunshin	Glasgow	RC
O'NEILL, James	35		Lisnahunshin	Glasgow	RC
O'NEILL, John	42		Lisnahunshin	Glasgow	RC
MOONEY, Neil	35		Carmagrim	Glasgow	RC
McFALL, Ennis	40		Carmagrim	Glasgow	RC
COLLINS, William	30		Kilcurry	Glasgow	P
McNEILLY, David	35		Kilcurry	Glasgow	P
YOUNG, Peter	30		Loan	Glasgow	P
McCOLLUM, James	22		Finkiltagh	Glasgow	P
McCOLLUM, Hugh	26		Finkiltagh	Glasgow	P
McINTYRE, Arthur	27		Carmagrim	Liverpool	RC
SCULLION, Henry	39		Carmagrim	Liverpool	RC
O'NEILL, Charles	23		Carmagrim	Liverpool	RC
KIELT, Daniel	30		Carmagrim	Liverpool	RC
O'HARA, James	34		Lisnahunshin	Glasgow	RC
MAXWELL, William	35		Tullygrally	Glasgow	P
CONAGHY, James	32		Tullygowan	Glasgow	P
CONAGHY, Alexander	35		Tullygowan	Glasgow	P
BOYLE, Daniel	25		Broughdone	Glasgow	RC
McCIBBIN, Robert	32		Broughdone	Glasgow	RC
McILRATH, Hugh	25		Ballyclosh	Glasgow	P
PATTERSON, William	40		Dunnygarr	Glasgow	P
MAY, Robert	32		Portglenone	Glasgow	EC

COUNTY: ANTRIM
PARISH: BALLYLINNY

NAME	AGE	YEAR LEFT	TOWNLAND	DESTINATION	TRADE	RELI-GION
MONTGOMERY, Jonathan	45	1836	Ballylinny	Quebec	Weaver	P
MONTGOMERY, Mary	40	1836	Ballylinny	Quebec		P
MONTGOMERY, John	16	1836	Ballylinny	Quebec	Weaver	P
MONTGOMERY, James	14	1836	Ballylinny	Quebec	Labourer	P
MONTGOMERY, William	12	1836	Ballylinny	Quebec	Labourer	P
BROWN, James	25	1836	Ballyearl	Philadelphia	Baker	P
BARRON, Thomas	26	1836	Ballyearl	Philadelphia	Baker	P
GAWLEY, James	25	1837	Carntall	Quebec	Weaver	P
MARTIN, Edward	22	1837	Carntall	Quebec	Weaver	P
MARTIN, James	14	1837	Carntall	Quebec	Weaver	P
McCAHEY, John	26	1837	Carntall	Quebec	Weaver	P
NEWELL, William	20	1837	Ballyearl	New York	Weaver	P
BLANE, John	18	1837	Ballyearl	New York	Labourer	P
WOODSIDE, Alexander	19	1837	Ballyearl	New York	Labourer	P
MARSHALL, Hugh	40	1837	Ballyearl	New York	Labourer	P
MARSHALL, Fanny	70	1837	Ballyearl	New York		P
GARDNER, William	20	1837	Ballyearl	New York	Labourer	P
MARSHALL, John	30	1837	Ballyearl	New York	Labourer	P
MARSHALL, Jane	21	1837	Ballyearl	New York		P

COUNTY: ANTRIM   SEASONAL MIGRANTS
PARISH: BALLYLINNY

NAME	AGE	YEAR LEFT	TOWNLAND	DESTINATION	TRADE	RELI-GION
MOORE, John	28		Ballylinny	Glasgow	Weaver	P
MOORE, Malcom	18		Ballylinny	Glasgow	Weaver	P

ORDNANCE SURVEY MEMOIRS

COUNTY: ANTRIM
PARISH: BALLYMARTIN

NAME	AGE	YEAR LEFT	TOWNLAND	DESTINATION	TRADE	RELI-GION
PARKER, Robert	40	1837	Carnanee	Philadelphia	Farmer	P

COUNTY: ANTRIM
PARISH: BALLYNURE

NAME	AGE	YEAR LEFT	TOWNLAND	DESTINATION	RELI-GION
McDOWELL, Thomas	24	1835	Ballynure	New York	M
McDOWELL, William	18	1836	Ballynure	New York	M
MOFFIT, William	50	1836	Ballynure	New York	P
MOFFIT, Ellen	40	1836	Ballynure	New York	P
MOFFIT, Eliza	18	1836	Ballynure	New York	P
MOFFIT, Sally	14	1836	Ballynure	New York	P
HUEY, Robert	22	1836	Ballynure	New York	P
MONTGOMERY, Robert	24	1836	Ballynure	New York	P
MONTGOMERY, James	18	1836	Ballynure	New York	P
MONTGOMERY, Jane	16	1836	Ballynure	New York	P
KAINE, Ellen	22	1836	Ballynure	New York	P
HUNTER, William	18	1836	Clements Hill	New York	P
HUNTER, John	20	1836	Clements Hill	New York	P

COUNTY: ANTRIM
PARISH: BALLYNURE

NAME	AGE	YEAR LEFT	TOWNLAND	DESTINATION	TRADE	RELI-GION
WILSON, Mary	60	1837	Ballylagan	Quebec		P
WILSON, John	19	1837	Ballylagan	Quebec	Farmer	P
McILROY, John	25	1837	Castletown	Quebec	Weaver	P
McILROY, Jane	20	1837	Castletown	Quebec		P
LOGAN, Matty	19	1838	Ballynure	New York	Weaver	P
MORELL, William	35	1838	Ballynure	New York	Cotton - Spinner	P
ROBINSON, William	20	1838	Ballynure	New York	Weaver	P
ROBINSON, Sally	20	1838	Ballynure	New York		P
ROBINSON, Samuel	16	1838	Ballynure	New York	Tailor	P
McCULLOCK, George	18	1839	Ballygowan	Quebec	Farmer	P
McCULLOCK, Jane	19	1839	Ballygowan	Quebec		P
COOK, Hugh	40	1839	Ballygowan	Quebec	Carpenter	P
COOK, William	20	1839	Ballygowan	Quebec	Farmer	P
ROBINSON, James	18	1839	Ballygowan	Quebec	Farmer	P
BELL, Mary	35	1839	Ballynarry	Quebec		P
BELL, David	14	1839	Ballynarry	Quebec	Labourer	P
BELL, John	12	1839	Ballynarry	Quebec	Labourer	P
BELL, Margaret	10	1839	Ballynarry	Quebec		P
McCORD, John	20	1839	Castletown	Quebec	Labourer	P
McCORD, Ellen	19	1839	Castletown	Quebec		P
McCORD, Samuel	1	1839	Castletown	Quebec		P
BURNS, Roger	30	1839	Ballynure	New York	Mechanic	P
HUEY, William	20	1839	Ballynure	New York	Mechanic	P
HUEY, Christiania	30	1839	Ballynure	New York		P
HUEY, Betty	28	1839	Ballynure	New York		P
HUEY, Margaret	24	1839	Ballynure	New York	Cotton - Spinner	P .
HATTIN, Hugh	17	1839	Ballynure	New York	Cotton - Spinner	P

COUNTY: ANTRIM
PARISH: BALLYRASHANE

NAME	AGE	YEAR LEFT	TOWNLAND	DESTINATION	RELI-GION
WILSON, Robert	23	1833	Lisnarick	Philadelphia	P
STEEL, William	20	1833	Carnglass	Philadelphia	P
STEEL, Adam	18	1834	Carnglass	Philadelphia	P
BLACK, James	19	1834	Carnglass	Philadelphia	P
CLARKE, Hugh	20	1834	Ballyrock South	Quebec	P
SMITH, Jane	50	1833	Risk	Quebec	P
SMITH, Margaret	22	1833	Risk	Quebec	P
SMITH, Jane Jun	20	1833	Risk	Quebec	P
SMITH, James	24	1833	Risk	Quebec	P
SMITH, Ann	26	1833	Risk	Quebec	P
SMITH, Samuel	15	1833	Risk	Quebec	P
NEILL, Jane	30	1834	Risk	Philadelphia	P
PATTON, Robert	27	1834	Risk	Philadelphia	P
PATTON, Ann	26	1834	Risk	Philadelphia	P
PATTON, Mathew	2	1834	Risk	Philadelphia	P
PATTON, Edward	6mths	1834	Risk	Philadelphia	P
PATTON, Mathew	18	1834	Risk	Philadelphia	P
McGOWEN, Hugh	26	1834	Outhill	Baltimore	P
PATTON, Thomas	19	1834	Ballywatt Leggs	Philadelphia	P
KILPATRICK, John	21	1834	Ballynatt Leggs	Philadelphia	P
NICKLE, James	24	1833	Revallagh North	Philadelphia	P

ORDNANCE SURVEY MEMOIRS

COUNTY: ANTRIM
PARISH: BALLYROBERT

NAME	AGE	YEAR LEFT	TOWNLAND	DESTINATION	RELI-GION
CLAWSON, Thomas	36	1836	Ballyrobert	New York	P
CLAWSON, Mary	35	1836	Ballyrobert	New York	P
REA, Matty	55	1837	Ballyrobert	New York	P
REA, Benjamin	20	1837	Ballyrobert	New York	P
REA, Samuel	22	1836	Ballyrobert	New York	P

COUNTY: ANTRIM
PARISH: BALLYSCULLION

NAME	AGE	YEAR LEFT	TOWNLAND	DESTINATION	RELIGION
McKOWEN, Rose	25	1835	Ardnaglass	Philadelphia	RC
REANEY, Ellen	18	1836	Gillistown	New York	P
CLARKE, John	36	1836	Gillistown	New York	P
McKOWEN, Catherine	32	1836	Kilvillis	New York	RC
CLARKE, John	9	1836	Kilvillis	New York	RC
JOHNSTONE, Robert	22	1836	Mill Quarter	Glasgow	EC
BOVEL, Thomas	28	1836	Mill Quarter	Glasgow	EC
BOVEL, William	35	1836	Mill Quarter	Glasgow	EC
McKOWEN, Bernard	35	1836	Ardnaglass		RC
DEVLIN, John	20	1836	Culnafay	New York	RC
LINSAY, John	23	1836	Taylorstown	New York	S
LINSAY, James	28	1836	Taylorstown	New York	S
GRAHAM, James	20	1836	Taylorstown	New York	BAP
LINSAY, Margaret	25	1836	Taylorstown	New York	P
McDOWELL, Josh	24	1836	Taylorstown	New York (Returned)	P
McDOWELL, Jane	31	1836	Gillistown	New York (Returned)	P
MURPHY, Andrew	25	1836	Taylorstown	New York	P
McDOWELL, James	30	1836	Gillistown	New York	P
DEVLIN, Arthur	23	1836	Taylorstown	New Orleans	RC
REANEY, Ellen	36	1836	Gillistown	New York	P
McKEOWN, Catherine	26	1836	Killylaes	New York	RC
CLARKE, John	10	1836	Killylaes	New York	P
BOVIL, William	30	1836	Mill Quarter	Glasgow	EC
BOVIL, Thomas	25	1836	Ardnaglass	Glasgow	EC
BOVIL, John	28	1836	Ardnaglass	Glasgow	EC
McALLEN, Sampson	50	1836	Mill Quarter	Glasgow	EC
McALLEN, Rachael	19	1836	Mill Quarter	Glasgow	EC
BOVIL, Eliza	20	1836	Mill Quarter	Glasgow	EC
BOVIL, John Jun (Died)	3	1836	Mill Quarter	Glasgow	EC
BOVIL, Rachael Jun	1	1836	Mill Quarter	Glasgow	EC
MURPHY, Andrew	25	1836	Grange Park	New York	P

COUNTY: ANTRIM
PARISH: BALLYSCULLION

NAME	AGE	YEAR LEFT	TOWNLAND	DESTINATION	RELI- GION
McKEE, Hugh	40		Ballyscullion	Glasgow	RC
McKEE, Archy	36		Ballyscullion	Glasgow	RC
McKEE, Patt	38		Ballyscullion	Glasgow	RC
McKEE, John	18		Ballyscullion	Glasgow	RC
TOOLE, Henry	20		Ballyscullion	Glasgow	RC
SCULLION, James	22		Ballyscullion	Glasgow	RC
McKEE, Reynold	30		Ballyscullion	Glasgow	RC
LAFFERTY, Hugh	27		Balyscullion	Glasgow	RC
McCUE, Joseph	36		Ballyscullion	Glasgow	RC
FEENEY, Michael	34		Ballyscullion	Glasgow	RC
HARDY, Hugh	30		Ballyscullion	Glasgow	RC
GUNNER, Thomas	30		Ardnaglass	Glasgow	RC
GORDON, Robert	25		Aghavary	Glasgow	RC
McFALLS, Charles	30		Aghavary	Glasgow	RC
McKOWEN, Bernard	35		Ardnaglass	Kelsea	RC
GUNNER, Thomas	28		Ardnaglass	Kelsea	RC

COUNTY: ANTRIM
PARISH: BALLYWILLIN

NAME	AGE	YEAR LEFT	TOWNLAND	DESTINATION	RELI-GION
SINCLAIR, Daniel	17	1833	Craigahul	Philadelphia	P
McHENRY, Archibald	20	1834	Craigahul	Philadelphia	P

COUNTY: ANTRIM
PARISH: BLARIS

NAME	AGE	YEAR LEFT	TOWNLAND	DESTINATION	RELI-GION
STRANNY, David	30	1835	Lisnagarvy	New York	RC
CUBIT, John	21	1835	Broughmore	New Orleans	EC
SPRIGGS, Felix	20	1835	Broughmore	New York	
CHAPMAN, William	24	1836	Lisnagarvy	New York	EC
CHAPMAN, Eliza	22	1836	Lisnagarvy	New York	EC
CHAPMAN, Jane	20	1836	Lisnagarvy	New York	EC
STRANNY, Mary	28	1836	Lisnagarvy	New York	RC
STRANNY, Mary	6	1836	Lisnagarvy	New York	RC
STRANNY, Ann	4	1836	Lisnagarvy	New York	RC
MURRY, Jane	24	1836	Lisnagarvy	New York	RC
McCAULA, Patrick	26	1836	Lisnagarvy	New York	RC
McCAULA, Mary	24	1836	Lisnagarvy	New York	RC
DRAKE, Francis	18	1836	Lisnagarvy	New York	EC
TOSH, Marcus	28	1836	Lisnagarvy	New York	RC
DRAKE, William	23	1836	Lisnagarvy	New York	EC
CORDBY, Patt	29	1836	Lisnagarvy	New York	RC

COUNTY: ANTRIM

PARISH: CARNMONEY

NAME	AGE	YEAR LEFT	TOWNLAND	DESTINATION	TRADE	RELI-GION
FULTON, David	25	1835	Jordanstown	New York (Returned 1837)	Carpenter	P
GARDNER, William	26	1836	Monkstown	Philadelphia	Labourer	P
JOHNSTONE, William	35	1836	Whiteabbey	Sydney	Labourer	P
JOHNSTONE, Margaret	30	1836	Whiteabbey	Sydney		P
JOHNSTONE, David	12	1836	Whiteabbey	Sydney		P
JOHNSTONE, Isabella	10	1836	Whiteabbey	Sydney		P
CLARKE, Edmond	50	1837	Whitehouse	New York	Callico Printer	EC
CLARKE, Margaret Sen	50	1837	Whitehouse	New York		EC
CLARKE, Thomas	23	1837	Whitehouse	New York	Printer	EC
CLARKE, Anne	26	1837	Whitehouse	New York		EC
CLARKE, Bell	30	1837	Whitehouse	New York		EC
CLARKE, Margaret	20	1837	Whitehouse	New York	Labourer	EC
CLARKE, Teressa	18	1837	Whitehouse	New York		EC
CLARKE, Betsy	15	1837	Whitehouse	New York		EC
CLARKE, Mary	13	1837	Whitehouse	New York		EC
CLARKE, Edmond	11	1837	Whitehouse	New York		EC
CLARKE, Catherine	9	1837	Whitehouse	New York		EC
MONTGOMERY, Hugh	20	1837	Ballycraigy	New York	Weaver	P
MONTGOMERY, Margaret	18	1837	Ballycraigy	New York		P
GRIMSHAW, Thomas	24	1837	Whitehouse	New York	Printer Proprietor	P
McCREARY, William	30	1838	Monkstown	New York	Farmer	P
JAMES, William	34	1838	Monkstown	Quebec	Callico Printer	P
McCOMBE, Nancy	30	1838	Croghfern	New York	Servant	P
CHISM, James	21	1838	Croghfern	New York	Farmer	P
BOYDE, Margaret	45	1838	Whitewells	Glasgow	None	P
BOYDE, Alexander	15	1838	Whitewells	Glasgow	None	P
BOYDE, Margaret Jun	13	1838	Whitewells	Glasgow	None	P
BOYDE, John	11	1838	Whitewells	Glasgow	None	P
BOYDE, William John	9	1838	Whitewells	Glasgow	None	P

COUNTY: ANTRIM
PARISH: CARNMONEY

NAME	AGE	YEAR LEFT	TOWNLAND	DESTINATION	TRADE	RELI-GION
McCONNELL, John	22		Whitehouse	Liverpool	Printer	EC
McCONNELL, William	20		Whitehouse	Glasgow	Printer	EC
JOHNSTONE, James	21		Monkstown	Glasgow	Printer	P
JOHNSTONE, William	19		Monkstown	Glasgow	Tailor	P
JOHNSTONE, Joseph	17		Monkstown	Glasgow	Printer	P
JOHNSTONE, Thomas	15		Monkstown	Glasgow	Printer	P
JOHNSTONE, Robert	13		Monkstown	Glasgow	Printer	P
JOHNSTONE, Archy	11		Monkstown	Glasgow	Printer	P

COUNTY: ANTRIM
PARISH: CARRICKFERGUS

NAME	AGE	YEAR LEFT	TOWNLAND	DESTINATION	TRADE	RELI-GION
McCANN, Ezekiel	66	1836	Carrickfergus	Quebec	Weaver	EC
McDOWELL, James	70	1836	Carrickfergus	Baltimore	Labourer	P
BURGOINE, Bridget	36	1836	Carrickfergus	Quebec		RC
MURRAY, Thomas	21	1836	Carrickfergus	New York	Blacksmith	P
MURRAY, Nancy	55	1836	Carrickfergus	New York		P
MURRAY, Nancy Jun	14	1836	Carrickfergus	New York		P
MURRAY, Samuel	19	1836	Carrickfergus	New York	Tailor	P
MURRAY, John	17	1836	Carrickfergus	New York	Tailor	P
MURRAY, Sarah	15	1836	Carrickfergus	New York		P
CONNOR, William	20	1836	Carrickfergus	Quebec	Labourer	RC
MOFFIT, William	55	1836	Carrickfergus	New York	Farmer	P
MOFFIT, Ellen	53	1836	Carrickfergus	New York		P
MOFFIT, Eliza	23	1836	Carrickfergus	New York		P
MOFFIT, Sarah	18	1836	Carrickfergus	New York		P
MOFFIT, Nancy	16	1836	Carrickfergus	New York		P
ERSKINE, Richard	60	1836	Carrickfergus	New York		P
ERSKINE, Anne	45	1836	Carrickfergus	New York		P
ERSKINE, Betty	20	1836	Carrickfergus	New York		P
ERSKINE, Margaret	25	1836	Carrickfergus	New York		P
ERSKINE, Richard	18	1836	Carrickfergus	New York		P
ERSKINE, William	16	1836	Carrickfergus	New York		P
ERSKINE, Robert	14	1836	Carrickfergus	New York		P
ERSKINE, Henry	12	1836	Carrickfergus	New York		P
ERSKINE, Jane	10	1836	Carrickfergus	New York		P
ERSKINE, Isabella	8	1836	Carrickfergus	New York		P
ERSKINE, Anne	6	1836	Carrickfergus	New York		P
CONNOR, William Jun	16	1836	Carrickfergus	New York	Labourer	P
McCULLEN, Henry	24	1836	Loughmourne	New York	Labourer	P
STUART, Agnes	20	1836	Loughmourne	New York	Weaver	COV
JUNKIN, Jane	18	1836	Loughmourne	New York		COV
JUNKIN, Betty	20	1836	Loughmourne	New York		COV
CONNORS, William	65	1836	Middle Division	New York	Labourer	P
CONNOR, Susana	60	1836	Middle Division	New York		RC
MILLER, Mary	30	1836	Middle Division	New York		
MILLER, James	28	1836	West Division	New York	Carpenter	P
CONNOR, Robert	20	1836	West Division	New York	Printer – Cotton	P
CONNOR, Archibald	18	1836	West Division	New York	Labourer	P
McDOWELL, William	37	1836	West Division	New York	Labourer	P
JAMISON, Thomas	35	1836	West Division	New York	Labourer	P
JAMISON, Anne	35	1836	West Division	New York		P
JAMISON, Jane	4	1836	West Division	New York		P
JAMISON, Janet	1	1836	West Division	New York		P
CAHEY, Arthur	20	1837	N.E. Division	Quebec	Labourer	P
LATTIMOR, Thomas	21	1837	Middle Division	Quebec	Labourer	P
MOFFIT, Robert	23	1837	Woodburn	New York	Blacksmith	P
CONNOR, Susana	15	1837	Middle Division	New York		P
MOFFIT, Agnus	3wks	1837	Middle Division	New York		P
McQUILLAN, Edward	27	1837	Carrickfergus	New York	Labourer	P
McDOWELL, Eliza	21	1837	Carrickfergus	New York		P
McDOWELL, Margaret	40	1837	Carrickfergus	New York		P
McDOWELL, Jane	26	1837	Carrickfergus	New York		P
McDOWELL, Ellen	16	1837	Carrickfergus	New York		P
KELL, Samuel	60	1838	Knockragh	Quebec	Farmer	P
SHEARER, James	21	1838	Carrickfergus	New York	Carman	P
McDOWELL, Ephriam	32	1838	Knockragh	Quebec	Weaver	P
McDOWELL, Jane	26	1838	Knockragh	Quebec	Weaver	P
McDOWELL, Matilda	7	1838	Knockragh	Quebec		P
McDOWELL, Margaret	5	1838	Knockragh	Quebec		P
McDOWELL, Mary Eliza	3	1838	Knockragh	Quebec		P
McDOWELL, Jane	1	1838	Knockragh	Quebec		P
WILSON, John	40	1838	Middle Division	Charlestown	Cotton –	P
WILSON, Nancy	30	1838	Middle Division	Charlestown	Spinners	P
McCORMICK, William	50	1838	Middle Division	New York	Cotton – Spinner	P

COUNTY: ANTRIM
PARISH: CARRICKFERGUS

NAME	AGE	YEAR LEFT	TOWNLAND	DESTINATION	TRADE	RELI-GION
McCORMICK, Jane	18	1838	Middle Division	New York	Cotton – Spinner	P
McCORMICK, James	14	1838	Middle Division	New York	Clerk in Mill	P
McCORMICK, Nancy	12	1838	Middle Division	New York	Dress Maker	P
GORDON, John	23	1838	Middle Division	New York	Blacksmith	P
McDOWELL, James	66	1838	Carrickfergus	New York	Farmer	P
McKEEN, John	22	1838	Carrickfergus	Quebec	Shoemaker	P

ORDNANCE SURVEY MEMOIRS

COUNTY: ANTRIM

SEASONAL MIGRANTS

PARISH: CARICKFERGUS

NAME	AGE	YEAR LEFT	TOWNLAND	DESTINATION	TRADE	RELI- GION
MULHOLLAND, Hugh	30		Torytown	Glasgow	Labourer	RC
MACAULEY, William	35		Torytown	Glasgow	Dyer	EC
GILLAND, William	35		Torytown	Glasgow	Printer	P
BAIRD, Andrew	25		Torytown	Glasgow	Labourer	RC
KEENAN, Joseph	30		Torytown	Glasgow	Printer	RC
KEENAN, William	24		Torytown	Glasgow	Labourer	RC
MULHOLLAND, Patrick	28		Loughmourne	Glasgow	Weaver	RC
NEILL, Alexander	18		Loughmourne	Glasgow	Weaver	RC
KILLIGAN, William	20		Loughmourne	Glasgow	Weaver	RC
PULLAN, George	24		Loughmourne	Glasgow	Weaver	P
MAGILL, William	34		Loughmourne	Glasgow	Weaver	P
MAGILL, Anne	26		Loughmourne	Glasgow		P
CLOSE, James	50		Carrickfergus	Liverpool	Labourer	RC
CREIGHTON, George	30		Knockragh	Glasgow	Labourer	P
MULHOLLAND, Peter	26		Western Division	Glasgow	Labourer	RC
HALL, Edward	20		Western Division	Whitehaven	Carman	P
MOFFIT, John	40		Western Division	Glasgow	Blacksmith	EC

23

COUNTY: ANTRIM
PARISH: CRANFIELD

NAME	AGE	YEAR LEFT	TOWNLAND	DESTINATION	RELI-GION
IRWIN, Edward	30	1835	Cranfield	New Orleans	P
HUME, Andrew	30	1835	Cranfield	New Orleans	P

COUNTY: ANTRIM
PARISH: CRANFIELD

SEASONAL MIGRANTS

NAME	AGE	YEAR LEFT	TOWNLAND	DESTINATION	RELI-GION
DUNCAN, John	23		Cranfield	Glasgow	RC
DUNCAN, Patrick	30		Cranfield	Glasgow	RC
McKOWEN, Charles	20		Cranfield	Glasgow	RC

COUNTY: ANTRIM
PARISH: DERRYAGHY

NAME	AGE	YEAR LEFT	TOWNLAND	DESTINATION	RELI-GION
STEWART, James	24	1835	Island Kelly	Quebec	EC
CLARKE, James	28	1835	Bovolcan	New York	EC
CLARKE, Mary	17	1835	Bovolcan	New York	EC
MILLER, Rebecca	25	1835	Bovolcan	New York	P
GALLAWAY, John	20	1835	Bovolcan	New York	P
GALLAWAY, Thomas	18	1835	Bovolcan	New York	P
HUNTER, William	52	1835	Killeaton	New York	P
HUNTER, Susan	35	1835	Killeaton	New York	P
HUNTER, Eliza	10	1835	Killeaton	New York	P
HUNTER, Mathew	12	1835	Killeaton	New York	P
HUNTER, Samuel	7	1835	Killeaton	New York	P
HUNTER, William	5	1835	Killeaton	New York	P
HUNTER, James	3	1835	Killeaton	New York	P
GALLWAY, Richard	17	1835	Magheralave	New York	P
DUNN, William	22	1835	Mullaghglass	New York	EC
DUNN, Adam	18	1835	Mullaghglass	New York	EC
DUNN, Alexander	20	1835	Mullaghglass	New York	EC
DUNN, Dally	16	1835	Mullaghglass	New York	EC
CROSSEN, Elizabeth	20	1835	Tornagrough	New York	RC
CROSSEN, Catherine	18	1835	Tornagrough	New York	RC

COUNTY: ANTRIM
PARISH: DOAGH

NAME	AGE	YEAR LEFT	TOWNLAND	DESTINATION	RELI-GION
KELLY, Samuel	20	1835	Ballyclare	New York	RC
ROBINSON, John	22	1835	Ballyclare	New York	P
QUINN, Alexander	19	1835	Ballyclare	New York	RC
MURDOCK, William	20	1835	Ballyclare	New York (Returned)	P
McBRIDE, Thomas	32	1835	Ballyclare	Philadelphia	P
ROBINSON, David	20	1836	Ballyclare	New York	P
ROBINSON, Joseph	24	1836	Ballyclare	New York	P
BEGGS, John	32	1836	Ballyclare	Quebec	P
BARON, Robert	20	1836	Ballyclare	New York	P
McBRIDE, Mary	10	1836	Ballyclare	Philadelphia	P
McBRIDE, Eliza	8	1836	Ballyclare	Philadelphia	P
McBRIDE, Nancy	6	1836	Ballyclare	Philadelphia	P

COUNTY: ANTRIM

SEASONAL MIGRANTS

PARISH: DOAGH

NAME	AGE	YEAR LEFT	TOWNLAND	DESTINATION	RELI- GION
NEESON, Titus	25		Ballyclare	Glasgow	RC
NEESON, Charles	20		Ballyclare	Glasgow	RC
McCRAY, William	30		Ballyclare	Glasgow	P
MORRISSON, John	24		Ballyclare	Glasgow	P
MILLER, James	25		Ballyclare	Glasgow	P

COUNTY: ANTRIM
PARISH: DRUMBEG

NAME	AGE	YEAR LEFT	TOWNLAND	DESTINATION	RELI-GION
SIMPSON, James	50	1835	Dunmurry	New York	P
SIMPSON, Mary	24	1835	Dunmurry	New York	P
SIMPSON, James	3	1835	Dunmurry	New York	P
CRAIG, Alexander	35	1835	Dunmurry	New York	P
CRAIG, Eliza	25	1835	Dunmurry	New York	P
CRAIG, William	6	1835	Dunmurry	New York	P
CRAIG, John	4	1835	Dunmurry	New York	P
CRAIG, Eliza	2	1835	Dunmurry	New York	P
CURTEAS, Edward	26	1835	Old Forge	New York	EC
FINLAY, Robert	30	1835	Old Forge	New York	P
FINLAY, Ann	28	1835	Old Forge	New York	P
FINLAY, Robert	8	1835	Old Forge	New York	P
FINLAY, James	6	1835	Old Forge	New York	P
FINLAY, Ann	4	1835	Old Forge	New York	P
COATS, William	28	1836	Ballyfinaghy	New York	EC
LYSTER, John	40	1836	Old Forge	New York	EC
HOOL, James	48	1836	Dunmurry	Quebec	EC
HOOL, Mary	46	1836	Dunmurry	Quebec	EC
HOOL, Robert	23	1836	Dunmurry	Quebec	EC
HOOL, James	21	1836	Dunmurry	Quebec	EC
HOOL, Jonas	18	1836	Dunmurry	Quebec	EC
CORR, Eliza	35	1836	Dunmurry	Quebec	EC
CORR, Mary	30	1836	Dunmurry	Quebec	EC
STEPHENSON, Thomas	50	1836	Old Forge	Quebec	P
STEPHENSON, William	23	1836	Old Forge	Quebec	P
STEPHENSON, Eliza	48	1836	Old Forge	Quebec	P
McGOLPEN, Agnes	68	1836	Old Forge	Quebec	P
GRAHAM, Margaret	22	1836	Old Forge	Quebec	P
McCULLOGH, William	21	1836	Old Forge	Quebec	P

COUNTY: ANTRIM
PARISH: DRUMMAUL

NAME	AGE	YEAR LEFT	TOWNLAND	DESTINATION	RELI-GION
NEESON, Charles	18	1835	Randalstown	Charlestown	EC
BAXTER, Elizabeth	21	1835	Maghereagh	New York	RC
BAXTER, Edward	25	1835	Magherreagh	New York	RC
BAXTER, Anne	¾	1835	Maghereagh	New York	RC
BAXTER, William	27	1835	Maghereagh	New York	RC
BAXTER, Bill	24	1835	Maghereagh	New York	RC
BAXTER, Martha	4	1836	Maghereagh	New York	RC
ENNISS, John	2	1835	Maghereagh	New York	RC
THOMPSON, Robert (Blacksmith)		1835			
McCLENAGHAN, Peter	30	1835	Lenagh	New York	RC
THOMPSON, George	20	1835	Aghaboy	New York	P
THOMPSON, Robert	20	1835	Aghaboy	New York	P
GLOVER, Jane	25	1835	Aghaboy	New York	P
HANAN, William	22	1835	Drumsough	New York	RC
HENDERSON, John	18	1835	Tamlaght	Charlestown	P
NICHOL, Hugh	20	1835	Ballydunmaul	New Orleans	P
WRIGHT, Catherine	21	1835	Ballydunmaul	New York	P
WRIGHT, James	19	1835	Ballydunmaul	New Orleans	S
HANNAH, William	22	1835	Drumsough	New York	RC
WALKER, John	55	1835	Terrygowan	New Orleans	P
WALKER, Mary	25	1835	Terrygowan	New Orleans	P
WALKER, Anne	21	1835	Terrygowan	New Orleans	P
WALKER, Margaret	23	1835	Terrygowan	New Orleans	P
CARSON, Thomas	21	1835	Terrygowan	New Orleans	P
COURTNEY, Samuel	18	1836	Randalstown	Charlestown	P
FRENCH, Martha	22	1836	Ballygrobby	New York	P
FRENCH, Mary	19	1836	Ballygrobby	New York	P
GILLILAND, James	24	1836	Ballygrobby	Quebec	EC
CARLTON, Thomas	18	1836	Clonboy	New York	EC
CARLTON, John	32	1836	Clonboy	New York	EC
CARLTON, Margaret	19	1836	Clonboy	New York	EC
MANORY, John	30	1836	Farlough	New Orleans	RC
MANORY, Mary	28	1836	Farlough	New Orleans	RC
WALKER, John	30	1836	Magherabeg	Glasgow	P
WALKER, Jane	32	1836	Magherabeg	Glasgow	P
THOMPSON, Mary Jane	13	1836	Maghereagh	New York	P
FARRELL, John	25	1836	Ballydunmaul	New York	P
FARRELL, Eliza	20	1836	Ballydunmaul	New York	P
MURRAY, Martha	18	1836	Ballydunmaul	New York	P
GRACE, John	26	1836	Ballealy	New York	EC
GRACE, Eliza	24	1836	Ballealy	New York	EC
KANE, Bernard	36	1836	Ballealy	Quebec	RC
MORGAN, Daniel	24	1836	Ballealy	Quebec	RC
CRAIG, Clara	24	1836	Clonboy	New York	RC
CRAIG, Catherine	22	1836	Clonboy	New York	RC
ROBINSON, John	27	1836	Clonboy	New York	P
TAYLOR, William	40	1837	Randalstown	New York	P
FRENCH, Sarah	17	1837	Ballygrobby	New York	P
LYONS, Thomas	22	1837	Maghereagh	Liverpool	RC
CRAIG, Catherine	19	1837	Clonboy	New York	RC
CRAIG, Clara	17	1837	Clonboy	New York	RC
HANNAH, John	60	1837	Lenagh	Quebec	P
HANNAH, Sarah	58	1837	Lenagh	Quebec	P
HANNAH, John	40	1837	Lenagh	Quebec	P
HANNAH, Hugh	38	1837	Lenagh	Quebec	P
HANNAH, James	36	1837	Lenagh	Quebec	P
HANNAH, Thomas	34	1837	Lenagh	Quebec	P
HANNAH, Margaret	32	1837	Lenagh	Quebec	P
HANNAH, Sarah	30	1837	Lenagh	Quebec	P
HANNAH, Anne	28	1837	Lenagh	Quebec	P
HANNAH, Eliza	26	1837	Lenagh	Quebec	P
HANNAH, Martha	36	1837	Lenagh	Quebec	P
KEILTY, Hugh	26	1837	Magheralane	New Orleans	RC

ORDNANCE SURVEY MEMOIRS

COUNTY: ANTRIM
PARISH: DRUMMAUL

NAME	AGE	YEAR LEFT	TOWNLAND	DESTINATION	RELI-GION
MACRORY, Charles	27	1837	Farlough	New Orleans	RC
MACRORY, Rose	18	1837	Farlough	New Orleans	RC
MACAULEY, Thomas	25	1837	Tamlaght	New York	P
GLOVER, Martha	25	1837	Aghaboy	New York	P
WATT, John	65	1837	Coolsythe	Charlestown	P
WATT, Eliza	22	1837	Coolsythe	Charlestown	P
WATT, Mary	20	1837	Coolsythe	Charlestown	P
WATT, Rose	18	1837	Coolsythe	Charlestown	P
WATT, Alice	16	1837	Coolsythe	Charlestown	P
WATT, John Jun	14	1837	Coolsythe	Charlestown	P
WATT, James	12	1837	Coolsythe	Charlestown	P
WATT, Jane	10	1837	Coolsythe	Charlestown	P
WATT, Sarah	8	1837	Coolsythe	Charlestown	P
IRVINE, William	28	1837	Coolsythe	Charlestown	P
LOUGHLIN, Eliza	26	1837	Tamlaght	New York	P
HOWARD, Samuel	38	1837	Coolsythe	New York	P
IRVINE, William	25	1837	Clare	New Orleans	P
McCRACKEN, Eliza	35	1837	Clare	Quebec	P
FOSTER, James	30	1837	Clare	Quebec	P
CARSON, Robert	25	1837	Procklis	New York	S
SMALL, John	25	1837	Ballymacilroy	New York	P
SMALL, Anne	20	1837	Ballymacilroy	New York	P
WEIR, Mary	18	1837	Ballymacilroy	New York	P
WEIR, John	16	1837	Ballymacilroy	New York	P
ALLEN, John	25	1837	Grogan	New York	P
TOOLE, Eliza	40	1837	Lurgan West	Glasgow	RC
KELLY, Martha	20	1837	Ballydunmaul	New Orleans	S
HERRILL, Eliza	27	1837	Ballydunmaul	St John	RC
HERRILL, John	30	1837	Ballydunmaul	St John	RC
HERRILL, Stewart	1mth	1837	Ballydunmaul	St John	RC

SEASONAL MIGRANTS

COUNTY: ANTRIM

PARISH: DRUMMAUL

NAME	AGE	YEAR LEFT	TOWNLAND	DESTINATION	RELIGION
KEILTY, Bernard	28		Magheralane	Glasgow	RC
KEILTY, John	24		Magheralane	Glasgow	RC
KEILTY, Bernard Jun	25		Magheralane	Glasgow	RC
YOUNG, Henry	22		Magheralane	Liverpool	RC
MARTIN, Daniel	28		Magheralane	Glasgow	RC
COOPER, John	50		Ballytresna	Glasgow	P
WATT, James	22		Ballytresna	Glasgow	P
SEYMOUR, William	22		Ballytresna	Glasgow	S
McILVENNY, William	35		Ballytresna	Glasgow	S
SANDYS, William	40		Tamlaght	Glasgow	MO
HINDMAN, John	30		Tamlaght	Glasgow	P
O'NEILL, Thomas	27		Aghaboy	Liverpool	RC
HOWARD, David	35		Coolsythe	Liverpool	P
HARPUR, Adam	40		Coolsythe	Liverpool	P
CAMERON, William	32		Coolsythe	Liverpool	P
CARSON, Andrew	35		Coolsythe	Liverpool	P
BRISTON, Harpur	40		Randalstown	Charlestown	P
MACRORY, Henry	34		Magheralane	Glasgow	RC
MACRORY, Hugh	20		Farlough	Glasgow	RC
MACRORY, Patrick	30		Magheralane	Glasgow	RC
MACRORY, John	26		Magheralane	Glasgow	RC
O'NEILL, John	32		Magheralane	Glasgow	RC
O'HARA, Arthur	20		Farlough	Glasgow	RC
COOPER, John	50		Ballytresna	Glasgow	P
WATT, James	22		Ballytresna	Glasgow	P
MACURBY, Edward	27		Tamlaght	Glasgow	RC
MORGAN, James	21		Tamlaght	Glasgow	RC
KNOX, John	18		Tamlaght	Glasgow	RC
ARMOUR, William	39		Coolsthe	Glasgow	P
REANEY, Hugh	30		Croggan	Glasgow	P
KENNEDY, Patrick	24		Croggan	Glasgow	RC
KENNEDY, Owen	31		Croggan	Glasgow	RC
McDONALD, James	21		Croggan	Glasgow	RC
NEELY, Thomas	24		Tannaghmore	Glasgow	P
NEELY, William John	26		Tannaghmore	Glasgow	P
McCARROLL, David	27		Tannaghmore	Glasgow	P
McCARROLL, James	29		Tannaghmore	Glasgow	P
McCARROLL, Thomas	22		Tannaghmore	Glasgow	P
McCARROLL, Robert	25		Tannaghmore	Glasgow	P
McCOMBS, Hugh	25		Tannaghmore	Glasgow	P
KINCADE, John	23		Tannaghmore	Glasgow	P
GILMOUR, Henry	25		Drumanaway	Glasgow	RC
MELON, Felix	33		Kilknock	Glasgow	RC
MELON, Henry	24		Kilknock	Glasgow	RC
McCANN, Patrick	22		Lurgan West	Glasgow	RC
POGUE, William	40		Ballynaleney	Glasgow	P
McKOWEN, Felix	30		Ballynaleney	Glasgow	RC
McANALLY, Henry	24		Ballynaleney	Glasgow	RC
McANALLY, Ephraim	40		Ballynaleney	Glasgow	RC
HOWARD, David	35		Coolsythe	Glasgow	P
HEANEY, Hugh	26		Leitrim	Glasgow	RC

ORDNANCE SURVEY MEMOIRS

COUNTY: ANTRIM
PARISH: DUNEANE

NAME	AGE	YEAR LEFT	TOWNLAND	DESTINATION	RELI-GION
McCLARNAN, James	30	1835	Moneyglass	Quebec	RC
McCLARNAN, Catherine	30	1835	Moneyglass	Quebec	RC
McCOART, Patrick	35	1835	Moneyglass	Quebec	RC
FERGUSON, William	25	1835	Ballymatoskery	Quebec	P
FERGUSON, Margaret	23	1835	Ballymatoskery	Quebec	P
FERGUSON, Jane	70	1835	Ballymatoskery	Quebec	P
MULHOLLAND, Mary	50	1835	Ballymatoskery	Quebec	RC
NEIL, John	23	1835	Tamnaghmore	New York(Returned Oct36)	
NEIL, Jane	20	1835	Tamnaghmore	New York(Returned Oct 36)	
MITCHELL, Henry	65	1835	Ballydonnelly	New York	P
MITCHELL, Margaret	64	1835	Ballydonnelly	New York	P
MITCHELL, Mary	25	1835	Ballydonnelly	New York	P
MITCHELL, Margaret	20	1835	Ballydonnelly	New York	P
MITCHELL, William	22	1835	Ballydonnelly	New York	P
COOKE, Esther	16	1835	Ballylenully	New York	P
MITCHELL, Robert	30	1835	Ballylenully	New York	P
BERRY, Elizabeth	20	1835	Lismacloskey	Quebec	RC
CUNNING, John	23	1835	Ranaghan	Quebec	RC
CONNOLLY, George	21	1835	Ballynafey	Quebec	RC
COOKE, Sally	40	1835	Ballydonnelly	Quebec	P
COOKE, William John	23	1835	Ballydonnelly	Quebec	P
COOKE, Sally Jun	6	1835	Ballydonnelly	Quebec	P
COOKE, William John Jun	4	1835	Ballydonnelly	Quebec	P
REANEY, Mary	22	1835	Moneyrod	New York	P
WILSON, Mary	20	1835	Moneyrod	New York	P
MUNDLE, Isabella (died)	18	1835	Moneyrod	New York	P
McINTYRE, John	18	1835	Moneynick	Boston	RC
McINTYRE, Ellen	16	1835	Moneynick	Boston	RC
McINTYRE, Margaret	20	1835	Moneynick	Boston	RC
MURPHY, George	25	1835	Derryhollagh	New York	RC
MURPHY, John	20	1835	Derryhollagh	New York	RC
NEILL, John	25	1835	Gortgill	New York	EC
NEILL, Peggy Jane	23	1835	Gortgill	New York	EC
COSTELLO, Henry	30	1835	Brecart	Glasgow	RC
McASTOCKER, Patrick	38	1835	Gortgill	Glasgow	RC
McASTOCKER, Catherine	40	1835	Gortgill	Glasgow	RC
McASTOCKER, David	12	1835	Gortgill	Glasgow	RC
McASTOCKER, Bridget	10	1835	Gortgill	Glasgow	RC
McASTOCKER, Mary Anne	8	1835	Gortgill	Glasgow	RC
McASTOCKER, Charles	6	1835	Gortgill	Glasgow	RC
McKOWEN, Hugh	20	1836	Carlane	New York	RC
MURPHY, William	45	1836	Derryhollagh	New York	P
MURPHY, Mary	34	1836	Derryhollagh	New York	P
MURPHY, George	16	1836	Derryhollagh	New York	P
MURPHY, Robert	18	1836	Derryhollagh	New York	P
MURPHY, Thomas	14	1836	Derryhollagh	New York	P
MURPHY, James	12	1836	Derryhollagh	New York	P
MURPHY, Mary Anne	10	1836	Derryhollagh	New York	P
MURPHY, Jane	8	1836	Derryhollagh	New York	P
MURPHY, Samuel	6	1836	Derryhollagh	New York	P
MURPHY, Robinson	4	1836	Derryhollagh	New York	P
LEVINGSTONE, Abram	20	1836	Derryhollagh	New York	P
McCORD, Margaret	20	1836	Derryhollagh	New York	P
McCORD, Robert	24	1836	Derryhollagh	New York	P
McCULLAGH, John	22	1836	Killyfast	Quebec	P
McCULLAGH, Anne	45	1836	Killyfast	Quebec	P
McCULLAGH, Jane	18	1836	Killyfast	Quebec	P
McCULLAGH, Levina	20	1836	Killyfast	Quebec	P
McCULLAGH, Eliza	16	1836	Killyfast	Quebec	P
IRWIN, David	45	1836	Moneyglass	Glasgow	EC
McKANE, William	22	1836	Ballymatoskery	New York	P
McKANE, Martha	20	1836	Ballymatoskery	New York	P
McKANE, Martha Jun	1	1836	Ballymatoskery	New York	P

COUNTY: ANTRIM
PARISH: DUNEANE

NAME	AGE	YEAR LEFT	TOWNLAND	DESTINATION	RELI-GION
DEVLIN, Patrick	31	1836	Ballynamullen	New York	RC
GRANT, Neil	40	1836	Carlane	Philadelphia	RC
CONOLLY, George	21	1836	Ballynafey	Philadelphia	RC
BAILY, William	21	1836	Tamnaderry	New York	P
GLOVER, Sally	20	1836	Drumboe	New York	P
MURPHY, William	50	1836	Derryhollagh	New York	P
MURPHY, Mary	35	1836	Derryhollagh	New York	P
MURPHY, Robert	18	1836	Derryhollagh	New York	P
MURPHY, Margaret	20	1836	Derryhollagh	New York	P
MURPHY, George	13	1836	Derryhollagh	New York	P
MURPHY, Thomas	11	1836	Derryhollagh	New York	P
MURPHY, James	9	1836	Derryhollagh	New York	P
MURPHY, Maryanne	7	1836	Derryhollagh	New York	P
MURPHY, Thomas Robinson	4	1836	Derryhollagh	New York	P
KING, William John	32	1836	Derrygowan	Quebec	P
KING, Hannah	24	1836	Derrygowan	Quebec	P
KING, Margaret Jane	2yr2m	1836	Derrygowan	Quebec	P

COUNTY: ANTRIM

SEASONAL MIGRANTS

PARISH: DUNEANE

NAME	AGE	YEAR LEFT	TOWNLAND	DESTINATION	RELI-GION
COSTELLO, John	20		Brecart	Glasgow	RC
McCLOSKEY, John	25		Brecart	Glasgow	RC
McBRIDE, Patrick	20		Brecart	Glasgow	RC
FRIEL, Hugh	25		Gloverstown	Liverpool	RC
McFARLAND, Robert	30		Gloverstown	Liverpool	P
BOYLE, Hugh	20		Gloverstown	Liverpool	RC
MALOWNEY, Andrew	20		Gloverstown	Liverpool	RC
MALOWNEY, Daniel	22		Gloverstown	Liverpool	RC
POLLOCK, William	26		Ballynaleaney	Glasgow	EC
McKOWEN, Felix	28		Ballynaleaney	Glasgow	RC
McANALLY, Henry	22		Ballynaleaney	Glasgow	RC
McANALLY, Abram	34		Ballynaleaney	Glasgow	RC
McCUE, Neal	35		Ballynaleaney	Glasgow	RC
BOYLE, Edward	35		Gallagh	Glasgow	RC
O'NEIL, Hugh	28		Aghacarnaghan	Glasgow	RC
O'NEIL, Henry	35		Aghacarnaghan	Glasgow	RC
MURRAY, John	28		Aghacarnaghan	Glasgow	RC
DEVLIN, Daniel	35		Aghacarnaghan	Glasgow	RC
McMULLAN, William	32		Cargin	Glasgow	RC
McMULLAN, Charles	36		Cargin	Glasgow	RC
McCANN, William	38		Ballynamullen	Glasgow	RC
McCORLEY, John	36		Tullaghbeg	Glasgow	RC
O'DONNELL, Henry	45		Tullaghbeg	Glasgow	RC
KENNEDY, Henry	38		Ballylurgan	Merryport	RC
O'NEILL, John	28		Carmorn	Glasgow	RC
DUNCAN, James	25		Moneynick	Glasgow	RC
GLASCO, James	30		Annaghmore	Glasgow	RC
POGUE, William	40		Ballynamullen	Glasgow	RC
MACUE, Patt	35		Ballynamullen	Glasgow	RC
McKOWEN, Felix	30		Ballynamullen	Glasgow	RC
FLURY, Rodger	24		Gortgil	Glasgow	RC
McBRIDE, Patt	20		Gortgill	Glasgow	RC
MAGILL, John	22		Gortgill	Glasgow	RC
O'NEILL, Frank	21		Gortgill	Glasgow	RC
CUDDEN, Frank	30		Gortgill	Glasgow	RC
McERLAIN, James	37		Gortgill	Glasgow	RC
SHIVERS, Henry	23		Gortgill	Glasgow	RC
McCANN, John	40		Gallagh	Glasgow	RC
McCANN, John Jun	30		Gallagh	Glasgow	RC
PHEA, Edward	40		Gallagh	Glasgow	RC
McMULLAN, William	29		Gallagh	Glasgow	RC
KENNEDY, Henry	53		Ballyduggenan	Glasgow	RC
McASTOCKER, Neil	21		Ballyduggenan	Glasgow	RC
BOYLE, Hugh	78		Lismacloskey	Liverpool	RC

ORDNANCE SURVEY MEMOIRS

COUNTY: ANTRIM
PARISH: GLYNN

NAME	AGE	YEAR LEFT	TOWNLAND	DESTINATION	TRADE	RELI-GION
MOORE, James	50	1839	Ballylig	Charlestown	Labourer	P
MOORE, Mary	45	1839	Ballylig	Charlestown		P
MOORE, Mary Jun	20	1839	Ballylig	Charlestown		P
MOORE, Jane	14	1839	Ballylig	Charlestown		P
MOORE, Samuel	12	1839	Ballylig	Charlestown		P
RUSKE, William	70	1839	Craignaboy	New York	Farmer	P
RUSKE, James	45	1839	Craignaboy	New York	Farmer	P
RUSKE, Wm Alexander Jun	19	1839	Craignaboy	New York	Painter	P
RUSKE, John	17	1839	Craignaboy	New York	Labourer	P
RUSKE, James Jun	15	1839	Craignaboy	New York	Labourer	P
RUSKE, William	38	1839	Craignaboy	New York	Farmer	P
RUSKE, Samuel	13	1839	Craignaboy	New York	Farmer	P
RUSKE, Samuel Jun	9mths	1839	Craignaboy	New York		P
RUSKE, Margaret	25	1839	Craignaboy	New York		P
WADDLE, Isaac	15	1839	Craignaboy	New York	Labourer	P
BLAIR, William	31	1839	Ballyvernstown	St John	Shoemaker	P
BLAIR, Jane	30	1839	Ballyvernstown	St John		P
BLAIR, William Jun	7	1839	Ballyvernstown	St John		P
BLAIR, Sarah	4	1839	Ballyvernstown	St John		P
BLAIR, Mary	2	1839	Ballyvernstown	St John		P
NICHOL, Patrick	18	1839	Ballyvernstown	New York	Labourer	P
McMURTRY, John	23	1839	Ballyhone	Quebec	Farmer	P
SHEARER, Mathew	16	1839	Ballyvernstown	New York	Labourer	P

COUNTY: ANTRIM
PARISH: ISLAND MAGEE

NAME	AGE	YEAR LEFT	TOWNLAND	DESTINATION	TRADE	RELI-GION
SAUNDERSON, Charlotte	20	1836	Gransha	New York		COV
ENGLISH, Thomas	50	1838	Portmuck	Quebec	Farmer	P
GILBERT, Jane	42	1838	Portmuck	Quebec		P
GILBERT, Nancy	54	1838	Portmuck	Quebec		P
GILBERT, Ellen	24	1838	Portmuck	Quebec		P
GILBERT, Thomas	36	1838	Portmuck	Quebec	Farmer	P
GILBERT, Thomas Jun	12	1838	Portmuck	Quebec	Farmer	P
COHEY, Samuel	36	1838	Portmuck	Quebec	Farmer	P
ESTLER, Eliza	8	1838	Portmuck	Quebec		P
ESTLER, Margaret	6	1838	Portmuck	Quebec		P
COHEY, Jane	1	1838	Portmuck	Quebec		P
PARKER, John	36	1838	Portmuck	Quebec	Farmer	P
PARKER, Mary	28	1838	Portmuck	Quebec		P
PARKER, Sally	5	1838	Portmuck	Quebec		P
PARKER, Anne	20	1838	Portmuck	Quebec		P
COHEY, Agnes	36	1838	Portmuck	Quebec		P
HARVEY, John	20	1839	Drumgurland	Quebec	Tailor	P
McCAULEY, Matty	25	1839		Quebec		P
PARKER, Mary	30	1839		Quebec		P
PARKER, Mary	8	1839		Quebec		P

COUNTY: ANTRIM
PARISH: ISLAND MAGEE

SEASONAL MIGRANTS

NAME	AGE	YEAR LEFT	TOWNLAND	DESTINATION	TRADE	RELI-GION
HUGHES, Henry	30		Cloughfin	Glasgow	Labourer	P
LOWES, Andrew	30		Cloughfin	Glasgow	Labourer	P
HUNTER, Andrew	26		Cloughfin	Glasgow	Labourer	P
DOFF, William	24		Cloughfin	Glasgow	Labourer	P
GREER, John	30		Cloughfin	Glasgow	Labourer	P
McMURTHRY, James	28		Cloughfin	Glasgow	Labourer	P
TEMPLETON, Robert	38		Ballylumford	Glasgow	Blacksmith	P
McALGORRAN, John	50		Ballylumford	Glasgow	Labourer	RC
GORDON, David	25		Ballylumford	Glasgow	Labourer	EC
MUNGLE, George	22		Ballylumford	Glasgow	Labourer	P
FEENY, Samuel	22		Ballylumford	Glasgow	Labourer	P
CREIGHTON, Patrick	28		Ballylumford	Glasgow	Labourer	P
DOFF, James	19		Ballylumford	Glasgow	Labourer	P
LAIRD, Anne	18		Gransha	Glasgow		P
MORELAND, William	38		Gransha	Glasgow	Labourer	P
McCAULEY, Thomas Brackirridge	17		Gransha	Glasgow	Labourer	P
STUART, William	25		Gransha	Glasgow	Labourer	P
LAIRD, Mary	20		Gransha	Glasgow	Labourer	P

ORDNANCE SURVEY MEMOIRS

COUNTY: ANTRIM

PARISH: KILBRIDE

SEASONAL MIGRANTS

NAME	AGE	YEAR LEFT	TOWNLAND	DESTINATION	RELI-GION
ARMSTRONG, James	20		Kilbride	Glasgow	M
STEER, Joseph	26		Kilbride	Glasgow	P
THOMPSON, Alexander	25		Kilbride	Glasgow	P

COUNTY: ANTRIM
PARISH: KILLEAD

NAME	AGE	YEAR LEFT	TOWNLAND	DESTINATION	RELI- GION
CHRISTIE, Andrew	21	1835	Ballyrobin	St. Andrews N.B. (Returned in 1838)	P
CHRISTIE, Samuel (Tailor)	27	1835	Ballyrobin	St. Andrews N.B.	P
McCUNE, George	38	1835	Dundesert	New York	P
McCUNE, Margaret	30	1835	Dundesert	New York	P
McCUNE, Fanny Anne	14	1835	Dundesert	New York	P
McCUNE, Ellina	12	1835	Dundesert	New York	P
McCUNE, Elleanor	10	1835	Dundesert	New York	P
McCUNE, Margaret	8	1835	Dundesert	New York	P
McCUNE, James	6	1835	Dundesert	New York	P
McCUNE, Mary Jane	4	1835	Dundesert	New York	P
OLLIVER, Robert William (School Master)	22	1835	Ballyrobin	Quebec	M
OLLIVER, Anne	35	1835	Ballyrobin	Quebec	M
DRENNAN, Joseph	21	1835	British	New York	P
OWENS, Robert	23	1835	British	New York (Returned)	P
McMULLIN, Thomas	65	1836	Ballyrobin	New York	P
McMULLIN, Agnes	60	1836	Ballyrobin	New York	P
McMULLIN, Alexander	28	1836	Ballyrobin	New York	P
McMULLIN, Mary	26	1836	Ballyrobin	New York	P
McMULLIN, Jane	24	1836	Ballyrobin	New York	P
McMULLIN, Anna	22	1836	Ballyrobin	New York	P
GILLESPIE, William John	22	1836	Seacash	New York	P
HADDOCK, Thomas	50	1836	Crosshill	New York	P
HADDOCK, Thomas Jun	22	1836	Crosshill	New York	P
HADDOCK, James	20	1836	Crosshill	New York	P
MONTGOMERY, James (Merchant)	24	1836	Straidhavern	New York	P
MONTGOMERY, Mary	21	1836	Straidhavern	Quebec	P
MONTGOMERY, Eliza	17	1836	Straidhavern	Quebec	P
MONTGOMERY, Robert	55	1836	Ballymather	Quebec	P
MONTGOMERY, Elizabeth	50	1836	Ballymather	Quebec	P
MONTGOMERY, Henry	15	1836	Ballymather	Quebec	P
MONTGOMERY, Catherine	18	1836	Ballymather	Quebec	P
MONTGOMERY, John	13	1836	Ballymather	Quebec	P
MONTGOMERY, Hugh	11	1836	Ballymather	Quebec	P
MONTGOMERY, Ellen	9	1836	Ballymather	Quebec	P
EVANS, Jane	21	1836	Kilcross	Quebec	P
EVANS, Stewart	19	1836	Kilcross	Quebec	P
REA, Samuel	26	1837	Crookedstone	New York	P
REA, Margaret	20	1837	Crookedstone	New York	P
McCARTHER, Catherine	30	1837	Dungonnell	New York	EC
CARLIN, Margaret	50	1837	Dungonnell	New York	RC
CARLIN, Margaret Jun	25	1837	Dungonnell	New York	RC
CARLIN, Nancy	20	1837	Dungonnell	New York	RC
GILCHRIST, Rev. Hugh Robert (Missionary)	24	1837	Ballyarnett	Australia	P

ORDNANCE SURVEY MEMOIRS

COUNTY: ANTRIM
PARISH: KILWAUGHTER

NAME	AGE	YEAR LEFT	TOWNLAND	DESTINATION	TRADE	RELI- GION
OGILBY, Samuel	24	1838	Headwood	New York	Labourer	P
BENN, Sally	26	1838	Headwood	Glasgow	Servant	P
MOORE, John	18	1839	Headwood	Quebec	Tailor	P
CLEMENTS, John	20	1839	Headwood	Quebec	Weaver	P
McCANN, Edward	25	1839	Craiginorne	Charlestown	Labourer	RC
WORKMAN, John	21	1839	Headwood	Charlestown	Farmer	P
WORKMAN, Mary	40	1839	Headwood	Charlestown		P
WORKMAN, Mary Jun	2	1839	Headwood	Charlestown		P
BOYD, Robert	20	1839	Lealies	New York	Blacksmith	P
BOYD, Eliza	19	1839	Lealies	New York		P
GILLAS, Samuel	29	1839	Lealies	Quebec	Farmer	P
GILLAS, Mary	25	1839	Lealies	Quebec		P
GILLAS, William	1	1839	Lealies	Quebec		P
GILLAS, Hannah	25	1839	Lealies	Quebec		P
MOORE, John	23	1839	Drumadonaghy	New York	Farmer	P
MOORE, Jane	23	1839	Drumadonaghy	New York		P
MOORE, William	1¼	1839	Drumadonaghy	New York		P
GILLAS, Robert	40	1839	Drumadonaghy	New York	Farmer	P
HAMILTON, Robert	28	1839	Lealies	Quebec	Schoolmaster	P
BELL, John	50	1839	Lealies	New York	Farmer	P
BROWN, Robert	25	1839	Lealies	Glasgow	Labourer	P
BROWN, Mary	24	1839	Lealies	Glasgow		P
BROWN, Mary Jun	4	1839	Lealies	Glasgow		P
BROWN, Ellen	2	1839	Lealies	Glasgow		P
BICKERSTAFF, John	30	1839	Headwood	Quebec	Farmer	P

COUNTY: ANTRIM   SEASONAL MIGRANTS
PARISH: KILWAUGHTER

NAME	AGE	YEAR LEFT	TOWNLAND	DESTINATION	TRADE	RELI-GION
COOK, John	23			Glasgow	Labourer	P
COOK, James	17			Glasgow	Labourer	P
COOK, William	24			Glasgow	Labourer	P
COOK, Andrew	20			Glasgow	Labourer	P
MORISSON, William	24			Glasgow	Labourer	P
MORISSON, John	25			Glasgow	Labourer	P
McILVENON, James	20		Mullaghsandall	Glasgow	Labourer	RC
McQUILLAN, John	18		Mullaghsandall	Glasgow	Labourer	P
McQUILLAN, Charles	26		Mullaghsandall	Glasgow	Labourer	P
WEIR, George	23		Bogtown	Glasgow	Labourer	P
AGNEW, William	30		Bogtown	Glasgow	Labourer	RC
AGNEW, James	27		Bogtown	Glasgow	Labourer	P
AGNEW, Daniel	25		Bogtown	Glasgow	Labourer	P
McILVENON, William	18		Bogtown	Glasgow	Labourer	RC
BANE, Joseph	25		Lealies	Glasgow	Weaver	P
BANE, John	21		Lealies	Glasgow	Servant	P
BANE, Robert	17		Lealies	Glasgow	Labourer	P
BANE, Sarah	22		Lealies	Glasgow	Servant	P
BIGGAM, John	27		Lealies	Glasgow	Millar	P
THOMPSON, Anne	20		Lealies	Glasgow		P

ORDNANCE SURVEY MEMOIRS

COUNTY: ANTRIM

PARISH: MAGHERAMISK

NAME	AGE	YEAR LEFT	TOWNLAND	DESTINATION	RELIGION
McAREAVEY, James	40	1835	Inisloughlin	New York	RC
McAREAVEY, Mary	36	1835	Inisloughlin	New York	RC
BOYES, Richard	25	1835	Maghaberry	New York	EC
GRAHAM, Francis	36	1835	Ballynalargy	New York	EC
GRAHAM, Rebecca	22	1835	Ballynalargy	New York	EC
HULL, Richard	24	1835	Magheramesk	New York	EC
HULL, Welsley	19	1835	Magheramesk	New York	EC
HULL, Matilda	21	1835	Magheramesk	New York	EC
HULL, Margaret	18	1835	Magheramesk	New York	EC
FEARY, Edward	30	1836	Maghaberry	New York	RC
FEARY, Catherine	28	1836	Maghaberry	New York	RC
FEARY, Mary	5	1836	Maghaberry	New York	RC
FEARY, Thomas	3	1836	Maghaberry	New York	RC
FEARY, William	1	1836	Maghaberry	New York	RC
HULL, Richard	20	1836	Maghaberry	New York	RC
DICKEY, James	45	1836	Maghaberry	New York	EC
DICKEY, Elizabeth	40	1836	Trummery	New York	EC
DICKEY, Bernard	20	1836	Trummery	New York	EC
DICKEY, Nathaniel	18	1836	Trummery	New York	EC
DICKEY, William	16	1836	Trummery	New York	EC
DICKEY, Robert	14	1836	Trummery	New York	EC
DICKEY, Debby	12	1836	Trummery	New York	EC
DICKEY, Mary	10	1836	Trummery	New York	EC
DICKEY, Norris	8	1836	Trummery	New York	EC
DICKEY, English	6	1836	Trummery	New York	EC
DICKEY, Elizabeth	4	1836	Trummery	New York	EC

ORDNANCE SURVEY MEMOIRS

COUNTY: ANTRIM

PARISH: MOLUSK

NAME	AGE	YEAR LEFT	TOWNLAND	DESTINATION	TRADE	RELI-GION
DUNLOP, Husband	35	1836		New York	Printer	
DUNLOP, Wife		1836		New York		
DUNLOP, Child	8	1836		New York		
DUNLOP, Child		1836		New York		
DUNLOP, Child		1836		New York		
McKELVEY, Margaret	23	1836		New York	Dressmaker	M

44

COUNTY: ANTRIM

PARISH: MUCKAMORE

NAME	AGE	YEAR LEFT	TOWNLAND	DESTINATION	TRADE	RELI-GION
McCANN, Patrick	30	1837	Old Stone	New York	Labourer	RC
McCANN, Hugh	28	1837	Old Stone	New York	Labourer	RC
JOHNSTONE, Martha	25	1837	Old Stone	New York		P
HARPUR, Margaret	20	1837	Old Stone	New York		P
HARPUR, Jane	44	1837	Old Stone	New York		P
ORR, Eliza	12	1837	Old Stoe	New York		P
McCANN, Mary	26	1837	Old Stone	New York		RC

ORDNANCE SURVEY MEMOIRS

COUNTY: ANTRIM
PARISH: MUCKAMORE

SEASONAL MIGRANTS

NAME	AGE	YEAR LEFT	TOWNLAND	DESTINATION	TRADE	RELI-GION
MURRAY, John	25		Old Stone	Glasgow	Labourer	RC
MURRAY, Neil	20		Old Stone	Glasgow	Labourer	RC
BEATTY, Henry	26		Shanoguestown	Glasgow	Labourer	P

COUNTY: ANTRIM
PARISH: NILTEEN

NAME	AGE	YEAR LEFT	TOWNLAND	DESTINATION	RELI-GION
BOYD, Robert	17	1837		New York	P

COUNTY: ANTRIM
PARISH: RALOO

NAME	AGE	YEAR LEFT	TOWNLAND	DESTINATION	TRADE	RELI-GION
DRUMMOND, William	25	1837	Ballygowan	Quebec	Labourer	P
CRAWFORD, James	60	1837	Ballyrickard	New York	Shoemaker	P
CRAWFORD, Mary	50	1837	Ballyrickard	New York		P
CRAWFORD, Joseph	24	1837	Ballyrickard	New York	Weaver	P
CRAWFORD, James	25	1837	Ballyrickard	New York	Weaver	P
CRAWFORD, William	18	1837	Ballyrickard	New York	Weaver	P
CRAWFORD, David	14	1837	Ballyrickard	New York		P
McAREEVY, Jane	24	1837	Ballyrickard	New York		RC
McWILLIAMS, Mary	44	1838	Ballyrickard	Charlestown		P
McWILLIAMS, Nathaniel	49	1838	Ballyrickard	Charlestown	Farmer	P
McWILLIAMS, Jane	14	1838	Ballyrickard	Charlestown		P
McWILLIAMS, Sarah	12	1838	Ballyrickard	Charlestown		P
McWILLIAMS, Nathaniel	8	1838	Ballyrickard	Charlestown		P
McWILLIAMS, William	4	1838	Ballyrickard	Charlestown		P
ROBINSON, Sarah	20	1838	Ballyrickard	Charlestown	Weaver	P
ASHTON, Robert	20	1838	Ballyrickard	Charlestown	Apothecary	P
ASHTON, Alexander	40	1838	Ballyrickard	Charlestown	Farmer	P
ASHTON, Jane	36	1838	Ballyrickard	Charlestown		P
ASHTON, James	14	1838	Ballyrickard	Charlestown		P
JUNKIN, Samuel	24	1838	Ballyrickard	Demerara*	Farmer	P
McWHIRTER, David	22	1838	Ballyrickard	Demerara*	Weaver	P
McADAM, Samuel	25	1838	Ballyryland	New York	Labourer	P
ROBINSON, Andy	24	1838	Ballyryland	New York	Labourer	P
McWHIRTER, Thomas	24	1838	Tureagh	New York	Labourer	P
ORR, Eliza	20	1839	Ballygowan	Quebec		P
McCORMICK, Jane	60	1839	Ballygowan	New York		RC
McCORMICK, Mathew	24	1839	Ballygowan	New York	Farmer	P
CRAIG, Robert	20	1839	Ballygowan	New York	Labourer	P
MOORE, Isabella	20	1839	Tureagh	Glasgow	School - Mistress	P
McDOWELL, Margaret	30	1839	Ballygowan	New York		P
DUNCAN, John	34	1839	Altilevelly	New York	Weaver	P
DAVISON, Nancy	32	1839	Altilevelly	New York	Servant	P
LOGAN, Eliza	22	1839	Altilevelly	New York	Servant	P
STUART, Charles	20	1839	Altilevelly	Glasgow	Labourer	P
PENNALL, Robert	21	1839	Ballyrickard	Demerara*	Farmer	P
SNODDY, Samuel	20	1839	Tureagh	New York	Tailor	P
FERGUSON, Margaret	20	1839	Bettia	New York		P

* Demerara (now Georgetown) is in Guyana

ORDNANCE SURVEY MEMOIRS

COUNTY: ANTRIM

SEASONAL MIGRANTS

PARISH: RALOO

NAME	AGE	YEAR LEFT	TOWNLAND	DESTINATION	TRADE	RELI- GION
GAULT, John	35		Ballygowan	Glasgow	Labourer	P
McFALL, Alexander	24		Ballygowan	Glasgow	Labourer	P
McFALL, Sally	35		Ballygowan	Glasgow		P
TIPPINS, Eliza	20		Ballygowan	Glasgow		P
GALLAGHER, Henry	25		Ballygowan	Glasgow	Labourer	RC

49

ORDNANCE SURVEY MEMOIRS

COUNTY: ANTRIM
PARISH: SHILVODAN

NAME	AGE	YEAR LEFT	TOWNLAND	DESTINATION	RELI-GION
DUFF, Thomas	15	1835	Tavnaghmore	New York	P
REDMOND, John	30	1835	Lisnevanagh	New York	P
SMITH, Patrick	40	1837	Tavnaghmore	Glasgow	RC
SMITH, Martha	40	1837	Tavnaghmore	Glasgow	RC
SMITH, Michael	4	1837	Tavnaghmore	Glasgow	RC
SMITH, Ellen Jane	2	1837	Tavnaghmore	Glasgow	RC
KELLY, Charles	26	1837	Tavnaghmore	New York	RC

COUNTY: ANTRIM

PARISH: SHILVODAN

NAME	AGE	YEAR LEFT	TOWNLAND	DESTINATION	RELI-GION
McKENNA, John	25		Tavnaghmore	Glasgow	RC
McKENNA, James	28		Tavnaghmore	Glasgow	RC
McKENNA, Patrick	38		Tavnaghmore	Glasgow	RC

ORDNANCE SURVEY MEMOIRS

COUNTY: ANTRIM
PARISH: TEMPLECORRAN

NAME	AGE	YEAR LEFT	TOWNLAND	DESTINATION	TRADE	RELI-GION
CREIGHTON, David	24	1836	Knocknagulliagh	New York	Mason	P
CREIGHTON, Jane	26	1836	Knocknagulliagh	New York		P
CREIGHTON, Mary	22	1836	Knocknagulliagh	New York		P
COWAN, Arthur	20	1836	Knocknagulliagh	New York	Labourer	P
WHYTE, Samuel	20	1836	Black Hill	New York	Carpenter	P
McMURRAN, James	22	1836	Lockstown	New York	Tailor	P
KINCART, James	25	1836	Lockstown	New York	Carpenter	P
BELL, James	25	1836	Ballycarry North West	Glasgow	Labourer	P
BUNTON, James	19	1837	Redhall	Quebec	Farmer	P
McCRACKEN, Thomas	27	1837	Redhall	Quebec	Labourer	P
McCRACKEN, Allen	25	1837	Redhall	Quebec	Labourer	P
MOATE, James	30	1837	Ballycarry	New York	Schoolmaster	P
McDOWELL, Robert	20	1837	Ballycarry	New York	Labourer	P
MOATE, Thomas	22	1837	Ballycarry	New York	Schoolmaster	P
McNEILL, Samuel	32	1838	Black Hill	Glasgow	Labourer	P
McNEILL, Nancy	32	1838	Black Hill	Glasgow		P
BELL, John	30	1838	Ballycarry	Glasgow	Labourer	P
ALLEN, Archy	32	1838	Ballycarry	Glasgow	Labourer	P

52

COUNTY: ANTRIM

SEASONAL MIGRANTS

PARISH: TEMPLECORRAN

NAME	AGE	YEAR LEFT	TOWNLAND	DESTINATION	TRADE	RELI-GION
ARMSTRONG, William	23		Ballycarry North West	Glasgow	Labourer	P
McMURTHRY, James	26		Ballycarry North West	Glasgow	Labourer	P
GREER, James	23		Ballycarry North West	Glasgow	Labourer	P
MORRISSON, Samuel	25		Ballycarry North West	Glasgow	Labourer	P
McKINSTRY, Samuel	40		Town of Templecorran	Glasgow	Labourer	P
McCUE, Frank	35		Town of Templecorran	Glasgow	Labourer	P

COUNTY: **ANTRIM**
PARISH: **TEMPLEPATRICK**

NAME	AGE	YEAR LEFT	TOWNLAND	DESTINATION	TRADE	RELI-GION
WILLIAMSON, Andrew	22	1835	Craigarogan	Van Demens Land	Farmer	P
WILLIAMSON, Jane	20	1835	Craigarogan	Van Demens Land		P
WILLIAMSON, Hannah	1	1835	Craigarogan	Van Demens Land		P
McBRIDE, David	22	1835	Craigarogan	Van Demens Land	Labourer	P
BROOKMIRE, John	25	1835	Craigarogan	New York	Printer	P
BROOKMIRE, Martha	15	1835	Craigarogan	New York		P
BROOKMIRE, Betty	24	1835	Craigarogan	New York		P
BROOKMIRE, Jane	22	1835	Craigarogan	New York		P
BROOKMIRE, Margaret	20	1835	Craigarogan	New York		P
BROOKMIRE, Isabella	60	1835	Craigarogan	New York		P
FEE, John	22	1835	Kilgreel	Glasgow		P
WILLIAMSON, Mary	34	1836	Kilgreel	Van Demens Land		P
WILLIAMSON, Jane	12	1836	Kilgreel	Van Demens Land		P
WILLIAMSON, Margaret Jun	10	1836	Kilgreel	Van Demens Land		P
WALKER, Thomas	25	1836	Kilgreel	Liverpool		S
HANNAH, John	25	1836	Kilgreel	Glasgow		P

ORDNANCE SURVEY MEMOIRS

COUNTY: ANTRIM

SEASONAL MIGRANTS

PARISH: TEMPLEPATRICK

NAME	AGE	YEAR LEFT	TOWNLAND	DESTINATION	TRADE	RELI-GION
JOHNSTONE, Frank	25		Craigarogan	Liverpool	Cotton-Printer	M
HAMILTON, William	30		Craigarogan	Liverpool	Cotton-Printer	M
BURGE, Patrick	60		Craigarogan	Liverpool	Cotton-Printer	RC
POLLOCK, Joseph	30		Craigarogan	Liverpool	Cotton-Printer	RC
HORNER, Isabella	27		Craigarogan	Glasgow	Cotton-Printer	P
CRAWFORD, William	32		Craigarogan	Glasgow	Cotton-Printer	M
McCLINTOCK, John	50		Craigarogan	Glasgow	Cotton-Printer	P
McCLINTOCK, John Jun	23		Craigarogan	Glasgow	Cotton-Printer	P
DEAN, William	26		Craigarogan	Glasgow	Cotton-Printer	P
PROW, Andrew	28		Craigarogan	Glasgow	Cotton-Printer	P
JOHNSTONE, John	20		Craigarogan	Glasgow	Cotton-Printer	M
JOHNSTONE, Frank	30		Craigarogan	Glasgow	Cotton-Printer	M
McLAUGHLIN, Gregor	22		Craigarogan	Glasgow	Cotton-Printer	RC
BYRNS, Thomas	22		Craigarogan	Glasgow	Cotton-Printer	P·
BALLIE, Adam	18		Ballynabarnish	Glasgow		P
BALLIE, Thomas	20		Ballynabarnish	Glasgow		P
HARPER, Samuel	23		Ballynabarnish	Glasgow		P

COUNTY: LONDONDERRY
PARISH: AGHADOWEY

NAME	AGE	YEAR LEFT	TOWNLAND	DESTINATION	RELI-GION
WALLACE, Margret	22	1834	Bovagh	Quebec	P
ORR, James	30	1834	Cullycapple	Quebec	P
ORR, Jane	32	1834	Cullycapple	Quebec	P
ORR, Margret Jane	11	1834	Cullycapple	Quebec	P
ORR, Eliza	9	1834	Cullycapple	Quebec	P
ORR, Ann	8	1834	Cullycapple	Quebec	P
ORR, Isabella	7	1834	Cullycapple	Quebec	P
ORR, Hannah	3	1834	Cullycapple	Quebec	P
MULLAN, Thomas	25	1834	Mullaghmore	Quebec	RC
MULLAN, John	30	1834	Mullaghmore	Quebec	RC
MULLAN, Bernard	23	1834	Mullaghmore	Quebec	RC
MULLAN, Cathrine	22	1834	Mullaghmore	Quebec	RC
MULLAN, John	20	1834	Mullaghmore	Quebec	RC
BOYLE, Patrick	20	1834	Glassgort	Quebec	RC
McFEETRIDGE, John	24	1834	Landagivey	Philadelphia	P
McGONIGLE, Margret	26	1834	Landagivey	Philadelphia	P
McGONIGLE, Mary	5	1834	Landagivey	Philadelphia	P
McGONIGLE, John	3	1834	Landagivey	Philadelphia	P
TRACY, Joseph	20	1834	Caleny	Quebec	RC
TRACY, Margret	21	1834	Caleny	Quebec	P
CANNING, Mary	30	1834	Caleny	Quebec	P
MAIRS, Sarah	40	1834	Ballyclough	Philadelphia	P
MAIRS, Margret	18	1834	Ballyclough	Philadelphia	P
MAIRS, Ann	14	1834	Ballyclough	Philadelphia	P
MAIRS, Sarah	12	1834	Ballyclough	Philadelphia	P
MAIRS, Jane	10	1834	Ballyclough	Philadelphia	P
MAIRS, Matilda	3	1834	Ballyclough	Philadelphia	P
MOON, John	25	1834	Clare Hill	Philadelphia	P
MOON, Johnathan	24	1834	Clare Hill	Philadelphia	P
MOON, Edward	20	1834	Clare Hill	Philadelphia	P
THOMPSON, Daniel	20	1834	Ballywillin	New York	P
YOUNG, William	35	1834	Shanlongford	Philadelphia	P
SMITH, John	20	1834	Moneycarrie	Philadelphia	P
JAMISON, Jane	19	1834	Aghadoey	Philadelphia	P
McALISTER, Andrew	40	1834	Keely	Quebec	P
McALISTER, Ann	38	1834	Keely	Quebec	P
McALISTER, Ann	16	1834	Keely	Quebec	P
McALISTER, Thomas	14	1834	Keely	Quebec	P
McALISTER, James	12	1834	Keely	Quebec	P
McALISTER, Margret	10	1834	Keely	Quebec	P
McALISTER, Robert	8	1834	Keely	Quebec	P
McALISTER, Susan	6	1834	Keely	Quebec	P
McALISTER, Mary	4	1834	Keely	Quebec	P
McALISTER, Andrew	2	1834	Keely	Quebec	P
McAFEE, Michael	24	1834	Keely	Quebec	RC
McAFEE, Martha	22	1834	Keely	Quebec	RC
McALISTER, Martha	50	1834	Dernacross	Quebec	P
McALISTER, Rebecca	18	1834	Dernacross	Quebec	P
McALISTER, Alexander	14	1834	Dernacross	Quebec	P
McNEIL, James	20	1834	Drumacrow	Quebec	P
FLEMING, John	21	1834	Gorran	New York	P
MOORE, James	22	1834	Ballynacally More	New York	P
MOORE, Izabella	21	1834	Ballynacally More	New York	P
WORKMAN, William	70	1834	Mullan	Quebec	P
WORKMAN, Mary	66	1834	Mullan	Quebec	P
WORKMAN, John	20	1834	Mullan	Quebec	P
WORKMAN, Richard	16	1834	Mullan	Quebec	P
WORKMAN, Margret	18	1834	Mullan	Quebec	P
McKEMINS, James	25	1834	Mullaghinch	New York	P
QUIN, Edward	20	1834	Meavemanougher	Quebec	RC
GILLON, Mary	45	1834	Meavemanougher	Quebec	RC
LOGUE, Patrick	16	1834	Meavemanougher	Quebec	RC
LOGUE, Ann	14	1834	Meavemanougher	Quebec	RC

COUNTY: LONDONDERRY

PARISH: AGHADOWEY

NAME	AGE	YEAR LEFT	TOWNLAND	DESTINATION	RELI- GION
PATTERSON, Samuel	33	1834	Clintagh	Philadelphia	P
PATTERSON, Elizabeth	25	1834	Clintagh	Philadelphia	P
PATTERSON, Joseph	62	1834	Clintagh	Philadelphia	P
PATTERSON, Richard	43	1834	Clintagh	Philadelphia	P
PATTERSON, Mary	26	1834	Clintagh	Philadelphia	P
STEWART, Margret	30	1834	Clintagh	St John	P
STEWART, Mary	4	1834	Clintagh	St John	P
MORRISON, James	20	1834	Crossmakeever	Quebec	P
KENEDY, Hugh	20	1834	Crossmakeever	Quebec	P
ADAMS, John	28	1834	Carranroe	Quebec	P
FULTON, Margret	18	1835	Ballyclough	Philadelphia	P
FULTON, Samuel	14	1835	Ballyclough	Philadelphia	P
FULTON, James	12	1835	Ballyclough	Philadelphia	P
FULTON, Mary Ann	10	1834	Ballyclough	Philadelphia	P
FULTON, Thomas	8	1834	Ballyclough	Philadelphia	P
FISHER, James	17	1835	Ballyclough	Philadelphia	P
FISHER, Samuel	19	1835	Ballyclough	Philadelphia	P
STEWART, John	19	1835	Crevolea	Philadelphia	P
TORRENS, David	20	1835	Crevolea	Quebec	P
McENTIRE, Robert	28	1835	Collins	Philadelphia	P
McFEETRIDGE, William	22	1835	Collins	Philadelphia	P
CANNING, David	24	1835	Collins	Philadelphia	P
SANDERSON, Thomas	22	1835	Collins	Philadelphia	P
COCHRAN, Andrew	24	1835	Ballinrees	Philadelphia	P
BARR, Samuel	28	1835	Seygorry	St John	P
BOYLE, Francis	40	1835	Cornamuclagh	Philadelphia	RC
BOYLE, Mary	30	1835	Cornamuclagh	Philadelphia	RC
LYNCH, Michael	40	1835	Kiltest	St John	RC
BROWN, Thomas	22	1835	Gortin	Philadelphia	P
McCLURG, Elizabeth	40	1835	Lisnamuck	New York	EC
McCLURG, Jane	16	1835	Lisnamuck	New York	EC
McCLURG, Archibald	14	1835	Lisnamuck	New York	EC
McCLURG, Jackson	10	1835	Lisnamuck	New York	EC
HEMPHILL, Hugh	27	1835	Ballybritain	Philadelphia	P
HENERY, Robert	22	1835	Lisboy	Philadelphia	P
McFAULL, James	30	1835	Ballynacally More	Quebec	P
BOYD, John	20	1835	Ballynacally More	New York	P
FREAM, Mary Jane	18	1835	Ballynacally More	New York	P
BOYD, Catherine	20	1835	Ballynacally More	New York	P
HILL, William	25	1835	Bovagh	New York	P
DOHERTY, Hannah	25	1835	Bovagh	Quebec	P
ADAMS, Elizabeth	8	1835	Bovagh	Quebec	P
McALICE, Michael	24	1835	Mullaghmore	Quebec	RC
McALICE, Elizabeth	22	1835	Mullaghmore	Quebec	RC
JAMISON, James	40	1835	Mullaghmore	Quebec	EC
JAMISON, Jane	30	1835	Mullaghmore	Quebec	EC
REID, Robert	60	1835	Managher	Philadelphia	P
REID, Ann	55	1835	Managher	Philadelphia	P
REID, John	21	1835	Managher	Philadelphia	P
REID, Miss	16	1835	Managher	Philadelphia	P
REID, Robert	60	1835	Managher	Quebec	P
REID, Sarah	52	1835	Managher	Quebec	P
REID, John	24	1835	Managher	Quebec	P
REID, Thomas	19	1835	Managher	Quebec	P
REID, Sarah	21	1835	Managher	Quebec	P
REID, Levy	16	1835	Managher	Quebec	P
ANDERSON, James	30	1835	Managher	Quebec	P
FULTON, Samuel	44	1835	Ballyclough	Philadelphia	P
FULTON, Mary Ann	42	1835	Ballyclough	Philadelphia	P
FULTON, Robert	20	1835	Ballyclough	Philadelphia	P
BOYD, Thomas	23	1835	Ballygawley	Philadelphia	P
BOYD, Esther	20	1835	Ballygawley	Philadelphia	P
KENEDY, William	25	1835	Ballygawley	Philadelphia	P
McNEIL, Robert	24	1835	Aghadowey	Philadelphia	P

COUNTY: LONDONDERRY

PARISH: AGHADOWEY

NAME	AGE	YEAR LEFT	TOWNLAND	DESTINATION	RELI-GION
HARKIN, Andrew	18	1835	Aghadowey	Philadelphia	P
BLAIR, Robert	50	1835	Aghadowey	Philadelphia	P
BLAIR, Rosey	48	1835	Aghadowey	Philadelphia	P
BLAIR, Joseph	20	1835	Aghadowey	Philadelphia	P
BLAIR, James	18	1835	Aghadowey	Philadelphia	P
RIDDLES, Robert	64	1835	Lisnamuck	Philadelphia	P
RIDDLES, Mary Ann	60	1835	Lisnamuck	Philadelphia	P
RIDDLES, Mary Ann	12	1835	Lisnamuck	Philadelphia	P
RIDDLES, Charles	20	1835	Lisnamuck	Philadelphia	P
RIDDLES, Elizabeth	41	1835	Lisnamuck	Philadelphia	P
RIDDLES, Matty	22	1835	Lisnamuck	Philadelphia	P
RIDDLES, Charles	40	1835	Lisnamuck	Philadelphia	P
RIDDLES, William	12	1835	Lisnamuck	Philadelphia	P
RIDDLES, Matilda	10	1835	Lisnamuck	Philadelphia	P
RIDDLES, Samuel	8	1835	Lisnamuck	Philadelphia	P
RIDDLES, Margret	6	1835	Lisnamuck	Philadelphia	P
RIDDLES, Robert	4	1835	Lisnamuck	Philadelphia	P
RIDDLES, Hugh	2	1835	Lisnamuck	Philadelphia	P
BOYES, James	40	1835	Lisnamuck	Philadelphia	P
BOYES, Ann	38	1835	Lisnamuck	Philadelphia	P
BOYES, John	18	1835	Lisnamuck	Philadelphia	P
BOYES, James	16	1835	Lisnamuck	Philadelphia	P
BOYES, David	12	1835	Lisnamuck	Philadelphia	P
BOYES, Leslie	10	1835	Lisnamuck	Philadelphia	P
CREITON, Ann	22	1835	Lisnamuck	Philadelphia	P
CREITON, Fanny	24	1835	Lisnamuck	Philadelphia	P
ROSBURG, John	17	1835	Lisnamuck	Philadelphia	P

COUNTY: LONDONDERRY
PARISH: AGHANLOO

NAME	AGE	YEAR LEFT	TOWNLAND	DESTINATION	RELI-GION
JOHNSTON, John	28	1834	Shanvey	Philadelphia	RC
JOHNSTON, Bridget	22	1834	Shanvey	Philadelphia	RC
GARVEN, Eliza	23	1834	Drumbane	Philadelphia	EC
HOPKINS, John	30	1834	Ballycastle	Quebec	EC
HOPKINS, Eliza	25	1834	Ballycastle	Quebec	EC
HOPKINS, James	10	1834	Ballycastle	Quebec	EC
HOPKINS, John Jun	8	1834	Ballycastle	Quebec	EC
HOPKINS, Matilda	6	1834	Ballycastle	Quebec	EC
HOPKINS, William	4	1834	Ballycastle	Quebec	EC
HOPKINS, Eliza Jun	2	1834	Ballycastle	Quebec	EC
THOMPSON, Hugh	20	1834	Ballycastle	Quebec	P
FERGUSON, Samuel	22	1833	Ballycastle	Quebec	P
GALLAGHER, Richard	20	1834	Carbullion	Quebec	RC
GALLAGHER, John	18	1834	Carbullion	Quebec	RC
MURTLAND, John	20	1834	Grannagh	Quebec	RC
MOORE, David	35	1834	Grannagh	Quebec	P
CONAWAY, James	30	1834	Grannagh	Quebec	P
SANDFORD, Mary	35	1833	Grannagh	Philadelphia	P
SIMEON, Mary	23	1833	Grannagh	Philadelphia	P
THOMPSON, Jacob	52	1834	Tullyarmon	Quebec	EC
THOMPSON, Jacob Jun	16	1834	Tullyarmon	Quebec	EC
THOMPSON, Anne	19	1834	Tullyarmon	Quebec	EC
THOMPSON, Mary	45	1834	Tullyarmon	Quebec	EC
HENRY, William	52	1834	Tullyarmon	Quebec	P
HENRY, Thomas	25	1834	Tullyarmon	Quebec	P
HENRY, Anne	50	1834	Tullyarmon	Quebec	P
HENRY, William	20	1833	Tullyarmon	Quebec	P
GARVEN, Mary	32	1834	Tullyarmon	Philadelphia	RC
DYSART, Rachael	24	1834	Tullyarmon	Philadelphia	RC
McLAUGHLIN, John	28	1833	Lisnagrib	Philadelphia	P
McLAUGHLIN, Jane	28	1833	Lisnagrib	Philadelphia	P
JOHNSTON, William	25	1833	Lisnagrib	Philadelphia	P
JOHNSTON, John	16	1833	Lisnagrib	Philadelphia	P
CONDLE, Mary	22	1833	Ballyhenry	Philadelphia	P
SMITH, Elizabeth	20	1833	Ballyhenry	Philadelphia	P
SMITH, John	21	1833	Ballyhenry	Philadelphia	P
MULLAN, James	20	1834	Grannagh	St John	RC
JOHNSTON, Jane	18	1834	Lisnagrib	Quebec	P

ORDNANCE SURVEY MEMOIRS

COUNTY: LONDONDERRY
PARISH: AGIVEY

NAME	AGE	YEAR LEFT	TOWNLAND	DESTINATION	RELI-GION
MULLAN, John	20	1834	Mullaghmore	Philadelphia	RC
MULLAN, Thomas	22	1834	Mullaghmore	Philadelphia	RC
MULLAN, John Sen	30	1834	Mullaghmore	Philadelphia	RC
HEGGARTY, Henry	25	1834	Mullaghmore	Quebec	RC
BOYLE, Daniel	19	1834	Mullaghmore	New York	RC
McSPARRAN, Letitia	26	1834	Lissaghmore	Quebec	P
BOYLE, Patrick	19	1834	Glasgort	Philadelphia	RC
McGONIGLE, Margaret	30	1834	Landagivey	Philadelphia	P
McGONIGLE, John	24	1834	Landagivey	Philaelphia	P
McGONIGLE, Mary	4	1834	Landagivey	Philadelphia	P
McGONIGLE, Jane	2	1834	Landagivey	Philadelphia	P
McFETRIDGE, John	22	1834	Landagivey	Philadelphia	P
MULLAN, Bernard	27	1835	Lissaghmore	New York	RC
MULLAN, Catherine	20	1835	Lissaghmore	New York	RC
MULLAN, Edward	3	1835	Lissaghmore	New York	RC
MULLAN, Catherine	1	1835	Lissaghmore	New York	RC
JAMESON, James	35	1835	Lissaghmore	New York	P
BYRNS, James	20	1835	Lissaghmore	New York	RC
DOGHERTY, Hannah	30	1835	Lissaghmore	Quebec	EC
McALEESE, Michael	20	1835	Lissaghmore	Philadelphia	EC
McALEESE, Elizabeth	21	1835	Lissaghmore	Philadelphia	EC
ELDER, Ellen	18	1835	Landagivey	Jamaica	P
MURRAY, Hugh	19	1835	Landagivey	Jamaica	RC
BYRN, Charles	24	1835	Mullaghmore	Glasgow	RC
DIAMOND, Daniel	60	1835	Landagivey	Glasgow	RC
DIAMOND, James	26	1835	Landagivey	Glasgow	RC
JAMESON, Jane	32	1835	Mullaghmore	Philadelphia	P
ROCKSBOROUGH, Martha	10	1835	Mullaghmore	Philadelphia	P

COUNTY: LONDONDERRY

PARISH: ARTREA

NAME	AGE	YEAR LEFT	TOWNLAND	DESTINATION	RELI-GION
HILLMAN, Henry	30	1834	Aughrim	New York	RC
HILLMAN, Herculus	17	1834	Aughrim	New York	RC
HILLMAN, Catherine	45	1834	Aughrim	New York	RC
HILLMAN, Elenor	20	1834	Aughrim	New York	RC
CONN, James	20	1834	Ballynenagh	Philadelphia	P
DONNELLY, Bridget	26	1834	Ballynenagh	Quebec	RC
GILMORE, Mary	21	1834	Ballynenagh	Philadelphia	P
RIDDAGH, Daniel	45	1834	Ballygruby	Quebec	P
RIDDAGH, Mary	42	1834	Ballygruby	Quebec	P
RIDDAGH, Jane	19	1834	Ballygruby	Quebec	P
RIDDAGH, Margret	21	1834	Ballygruby	Quebec	P
RIDDAGH, Sarah	24	1834	Ballygruby	Quebec	P
RIDDAGH, Ann	20	1834	Ballygruby	Quebec	P
RIDDAGH, James	10	1834	Ballygruby	Quebec	P
RIDDAGH, Mary	8	1834	Ballygruby	Quebec	P
RIDDAGH, John	6	1834	Ballygruby	Quebec	P
CASSIDY, Robert	24	1834	Ballygruby	Quebec	RC
McGANARTY, Edward	20	1834	Mawilliam	Philadelphia	RC
McGANARTY, Mary	18	1834	Mawilliam	Philadelphia	RC
McKEON, Charles	27	1834	Mawilliam	Quebec	RC
McKEON, Catherine	18	1834	Mawilliam	Quebec	RC
WALKER, Manual	21	1834	Ballindrum	Quebec	P
WALKER, William	19	1834	Ballindrum	Quebec	P
O'NEILL, James	40	1834	Ballygillen More	New York	RC
O'NEILL, Mary	40	1834	Ballygillen More	New York	RC
O'NEILL, Daniel	12	1834	Ballygillen More	New York	RC
McKEON, Murtagh	19	1835	Ballymulderg More	New York	RC
HANVEY, Edward	17	1835	Drumenagh	Philadelphia	RC
HANVEY, Sarah	23	1835	Drumenagh	Philadelphia	RC
HANVEY, Mary	25	1835	Aughrim	New York	RC
DIMOND, Paul	25	1835	Aughrim	New York	RC
DIMOND, Susana	35	1835	Aughrim	New York	RC
DIMOND, John	22	1835	Aughrim	New York	RC
DEVLIN, Sarah	20	1835	Aughrim	New York	RC
EDWARD, Samuel	20	1835	Derrygarve	New York	P
DEVLIN, Joseph	40	1835	Ballyriff	Philadelphia	RC
McCULLAGH, Bernard	26	1835	Mawilliam	Philadelphia	P
DEVLIN, Catherine	25	1835	Mawilliam	Philadelphia	RC
MULHOLLAND, Ann	26	1835	Ballindrum	Quebec	RC
McFILLEN, Sarah	30	1835	Tralee	Philadelphia	RC
SHEPPARD, Margret	17	1835	Tralee	Philadelphia	RC
DEVLIN, Sarah	35	1835	Tralee	Philadelphia	RC
GILMORE, Jane	15	1835	Ballynewry	Quebec	P
DALEY, Margrett	24	1835	Ballynewry	Quebec	P
RIGHT, Elenor	30	1835	Ballynewry	Quebec	EC
STITT, James	30	1835	Maghadone	New York	P
COSTELLO, William	32	1835	Ballygillen Beg	New York	RC
GILMORE, James	36	1835	Ballygillen More	New York	P
GILMORE, Mary	30	1835	Ballygillen More	New York	P
GILMORE, David	6	1835	Ballygillen More	New York	P
GILMORE, James	4	1835	Ballygillen More	New York	P
GILMORE, Ann	2	1835	Ballygillen More	New York	P
McGURK, Ann	30	1835	Moneymore	Quebec	RC
JOHNSTONE, Robert	20	1835	Moneymore	Quebec	P

COUNTY: LONDONDERRY
PARISH: BALLYAGHRAN

NAME	AGE	YEAR LEFT	TOWNLAND	DESTINATION	RELI-GION
McINTYRE, Hugh	60	1834	Kiltinny Beg	New York	S
McINTYRE, James	35	1834	Kiltinny Beg	New York	S
McINTYRE, David	18	1834	Kiltinny Beg	New York	S
McINTYRE, Esther	20	1834	Kiltinny Beg	New York	S
KEATH, Issac	33	1834	Craigtown More	Quebec	S
McALISTER, Duncan	27	1834	Bellemont	Quebec	S
McALISTER, Sarah	26	1834	Bellemont	Quebec	S
McALISTER, James	18wks	1834	Bellemont	Quebec	S
LUSK, John	19	1834	Bellemont	Quebec	S
KANE, John	18	1834	Bellemont	New York	S
MORRISSON, Archibald	35	1834	Kiltinny More	Philadelphia	S
MORRISSON, Jane	25	1834	Kiltinny More	Philadelphia	S
MORRISSON, William	6	1834	Kiltinny More	Philadelphia	S
MORRISSON, Elizabeth	4	1834	Kiltinny More	Philadelphia	S
MORRISSON, Matilda	2	1834	Kiltinny More	Philadelphia	S
DAVISON, John	20	1834	Garbogle	Quebec	EC
SHAW, Neil	35	1834	Mullaghacall	Quebec	P
SHAW, Martha	34	1834	Mullaghacall	Quebec	P
SHAW, Margaret	18	1834	Mullaghacall	Quebec	P
KERR, James	40	1834	Roselick Beg	Quebec	P
KERR, Mary	36	1834	Roselick Beg	Quebec	P
KERR, Nancy	9	1834	Roselick Beg	Quebec	P
KERR, Martha	7	1834	Roselick Beg	Quebec	P
KERR, Jane	3	1834	Roselick Beg	Quebec	P
KERR, Rachael	1½	1834	Roselick Beg	Quebec	P
ANDREWS, William	24	1834	Roselick Beg	Quebec	P
MILLER, David	25	1834	Roselick Beg	Quebec	P
KEARNEY, William	24	1834	Roselick Beg	Quebec	P
McINTYRE, John	22	1833	Kiltinny Beg	New York	S
HENRY, John	27	1833	Kiltinny Beg	Philadelphia	S
MORNING, James	30	1833	Kiltinny More	Quebec	P
MORNING, Margaret	26	1833	Kiltinny More	Quebec	P
MORNING, Elizabeth	12	1833	Kiltinny More	Quebec	P
BOYD, Thomas	30	1833	Kiltinny More	Quebec	P
BOYD, Ellen	28	1833	Kiltinny More	Quebec	P
BOYD, Margaret Jun	6mths	1833	Kiltinny More	Quebec	P
BRADLEY, Anne	19	1833	Drumslade	Quebec	RC
COCHRAN, Hugh	27	1833	Bellemont	New York	P
MEATHERS, Robert	50	1833	Bellemont North	Philadelphia (returned 1833)	P
McCAHAN, James	30	1833	Bellemont North	Quebec	P
McALISTER, John	36	1833	Islandtasserty	Quebec	P
McINTYRE, Hugh	25	1833	Islandtasserty	St John	S
NEVIN, Hugh	20	1833	Bellemont	Quebec (returned 1833)	P
MURDOCK, John	21	1833	Ballyleese	Quebec	P
McKINLASS, Samuel	25	1833	Craigtown Beg	Quebec	P
McKINLASS, Elizabeth	24	1833	Craigtown Beg	Quebec	P
BROWN, Alexander	50	1834	Ballygelagh West	Philadelphia	P
WALKER, John	50	1834	Ballygelagh East	Quebec	P
WALKER, Samuel	18	1834	Ballygelagh East	Jamaica	P
BAIRD, Jonathan	56	1834	Maddybenny	Scotland (returned 1834)	P
DOHERTY, Joseph	20	1834	Ballyleese	Quebec	P
DOHERTY, Sarah	25	1834	Drumslade	Quebec	P
WALKER, Jane	37	1834	Ballygelagh West	Quebec	P
WALKER, John	14	1834	Ballygelagh West	Quebec	P
WALKER, James	12	1834	Ballygelagh West	Quebec	P

ORDNANCE SURVEY MEMOIRS

COUNTY: LONDONDERRY
PARISH: BALLYNASCREEN

NAME	AGE	YEAR LEFT	TOWNLAND	DESTINATION	RELI-GION
REID, James	30	1834	Glebe	Quebec	RC
HENERY, Patt	24	1834	Disert	New York	RC
CONNERY, Charles	24	1834	Disert	New York	RC
O'NEILL, Charles	24	1834	Disert	New York	RC
O'NEILL, Bridget	26	1834	Disert	New York	RC
MORRIN, Thomas	24	1834	Disert	New York	RC
KELLY, Sophia	40	1834	Corick	New York	RC
KELLY, Mary	43	1834	Corick	New York	RC
Kane, Michael	18	1834	Drumard	New York	RC
ROBERTSON, Robert	21	1834	Drumard	New York	EC
GIBSON, George	24	1834	Drumard	New York	EC
GIBSON, Thomas	21	1834	Drumard	New York	EC
LEECH, Andrew	30	1834	Drumard	New York	EC
BRADLEY, Rosey	26	1834	Cloughfin	Quebec	RC
BRADLEY, Joseph	25	1834	Cloughfin	Quebec	RC
McNEILL, Elenor	30	1834	Cloughfin	Quebec	RC
GILLON, Domnick	32	1834	Moneyconey	Quebec	RC
SARGENT, Sally	20	1835	Mulnavoo	Quebec	EC
BRADLEY, James	25	1835	Glebe	Quebec	RC
BRADLEY, Elenor	22	1835	Glebe	Quebec	RC
HENERY, John	19	1835	Disert	New York	RC
CONNERY, John	20	1835	Disert	New York	RC
DONNELLY, Patrick	30	1835	Straw	New York	RC
DONNELLY, James	20	1835	Straw	New York	RC
McNALLY, John	30	1835	Moyard	Philadelphia	RC
CONNELLY, Patrick	25	1835	Moneyconey	New York	RC
BRADLEY, James	24	1835	Moneyconey	New York	RC
KELLY, Martha	35	1835	Corick	New York	RC
KELLY, Ann	5	1835	Corick	New York	RC
KELLY, James	2	1835	Corick	New York	RC

ORDNANCE SURVEY MEMOIRS

COUNTY: LONDONDERRY
PARISH: BALLYRASHANE

NAME	AGE	YEAR LEFT	TOWNLAND	DESTINATION	RELI-GION
McBRIDE, Robert	45	1833	Ballindreen Scotch	Quebec	P
McBRIDE, Mary	40	1833	Ballindreen Scotch	Quebec	P
McBRIDE, Mary Jun	22	1833	Ballindreen Scotch	Quebec	P
McBRIDE, Jane	19	1833	Ballindreen Scotch	Quebec	P
McBRIDE, John	24	1833	Ballindreen Scotch	Quebec	P
McBRIDE, Robert	17	1833	Ballindreen Scotch	Quebec	P
McBRIDE, James	15	1833	Ballindreen Scotch	Quebec	P
STEEL, William	24	1833	Ballyvelton Upper	Philadelphia	P
McENTIRE, Robert	20	1833	Ballyvelton Lower	Philadelphia	P
FERGUSON, Elizabeth	50	1833	Knocknakeeragh	Quebec	P
FERGUSON, Martha	20	1833	Knocknakeeragh	Quebec	P
FERGUSON, Margaret	18	1833	Knocknakeeragh	Quebec	P
FERGUSON, Mary	16	1833	Knocknakeeragh	Quebec	P
FERGUSON, Rosey	14	1833	Knocknakeeragh	Quebec	P
McELCUMNA, James	23	1833	Knocknakeeragh	Quebec	P
ROBINSON, Daniel	18	1833	Knocknakeeragh	New York	P
FERGUSON, Elenor	26	1833	Knocknakeeragh	New York	P
FERGUSON, Jane	30	1833	Knocknakeeragh	New York	P
STERLING, Thomas	20	1833	Kirkistown	Quebec	P
STERLING, William John	16	1834	Kirkistown	Quebec	P
BURNETT, Sinclair	20	1834	Cloyfin South	Quebec	P
McMULLEN, John	20	1833	Cloyfin South	Quebec	P
BOYD, John	19	1833	Cloyfin South	Philadelphia	P
WALKER, Hugh	21	1833	Ballyversall	Philadelphia	P
HYNDS, Martha	22	1833	Gorticloghan	Philadelphia	P
HYNDS, Margaret	3	1833	Gorticloghan	Philadelphia	P

COUNTY: LONDONDERRY
PARISH: BALLYSCULLION

NAME	AGE	YEAR LEFT	TOWNLAND	DESTINATION	RELI-GION
McCAHY, Samuel	50	1834	Ballyscullion West	St John	P
McCAHY, Jane	48	1834	Ballyscullion West	St John	P
McCAHY, Ann	25	1834	Ballyscullion West	St John	P
McCAHY, Margret	20	1834	Ballyscullion West	St John	P
McCAHY, John	18	1834	Ballyscullion West	St John	P
McCAHY, Elenor	16	1834	Ballyscullion West	St John	P
McCAHY, Jane	12	1834	Ballyscullion West	St John	P
McCAHY, Charles	14	1834	Ballyscullion West	St John	P
McCAHY, Sarah	6	1834	Ballyscullion West	St John	P
ADAMS, Samuel	25	1834	Ballyscullion West	St John	P
ADAMS, Jane	23	1834	Ballyscullion West	St John	P
SCULLION, Daniel	20	1834	Ballyscullion West	St John	RC
MULLAN, Jane	20	1834	Old Town Deer Park	St John	EC
VANCE, Mary	21	1834	Ballynacombs More	Quebec	P
VANCE, Catherine	24	1834	Ballynacombs More	Quebec	P
GODFREY, John	24	1834	Ballynacombs More	Quebec	P
GODFREY, Ann	22	1834	Ballynacombs More	Quebec	P
GODFREY, Rowland	26	1834	Ballynacombs More	Quebec	P
RICE, Mary	60	1834	Tamlaghtduff	Quebec	EC
RICE, Mary	30	1834	Tamlaghtduff	Quebec	EC
RICE, Ann	20	1834	Tamlaghtduff	Quebec	EC
RICE, Catherine	18	1834	Tamlaghtduff	Quebec	EC
RICE, Robert	22	1834	Tamlaghtduff	Quebec	EC
RICE, Robert	5	1834	Tamlaghtduff	Quebec	EC
RICE, Mary	7	1834	Tamlaghtduff	Quebec	EC
RICE, Ann	3	1834	Tamlaghtduff	Quebec	EC
McWILLIAMS, Elenor	30	1834	Tamniaran	New York	RC
McWILLIAMS, John	3	1834	Tamniaran	New York	RC
DIMOND, Ann	26	1834	Ballyneasa Strain	New York	RC
LOWDEN, Mary	20	1834	Bellaghy	New York	RC
BRADLEY, James	12	1835	Leitrim	St John	RC
BRADLEY, Izabella	32	1835	Leitrim	St John	RC
BRADLEY, James	3	1835	Leitrim	St John	RC
DOBBINGS, William	40	1835	Edenreagh	New York	P
DOBBINGS, Ezekil	19	1835	Edenreagh	New York	P
DOBBINGS, James	16	1835	Edenreagh	New York	P
DOBBINGS, William	12	1835	Edenreagh	New York	P
DOBBINGS, Henry	10	1835	Edenreagh	New York	P
DOBBINGS, Robert	8	1835	Edenreagh	New York	P
DOBBINGS, Isias	3	1835	Edenreagh	New York	P
FINNIGAN, Michael	30	1835	Edenreagh	New York	EC
FINNIGAN, Eliza	25	1835	Edenreagh	New York	EC
DIXON, Francis	40	1835	Ballynacombs More	St John	P
DIXON, William	30	1835	Ballynacombs More	St John	P
DIXON, John	28	1835	Ballynacombs More	St John	P
McCULLAN, Alexander	25	1835	Ballynacombs More	Quebec	P
VANCE, William	28	1835	Ballynacombs More	Quebec	P
VANCE, William	21	1835	Ballynacombs More	Quebec	P
CULLION, Jane	20	1835	Tamlaghtduff	Quebec	RC
DIXON, Margret	30	1835	Ballynacombs Beg	Quebec	EC
MULHOLLAND, John	24	1835	Ballynease Strain	New York	RC
BRADLEY, Eliza	40	1835	Bellaghy	New York	RC
BRADLEY, James	3	1835	Bellaghy	New York	RC
BRADLEY, James	13	1835	Bellaghy	New York	RC

COUNTY: LONDONDERRY
PARISH: BALLYWILLIN

NAME	AGE	YEAR LEFT	TOWNLAND	DESTINATION	RELI-GION
BROWN, John	24	1834	Ballylagan	Quebec	P
BROWN, Sarah	26	1834	Ballylagan	Quebec	P
BROWN, Mary	4	1834	Ballylagan	Quebec	P
BROWN, Nancy	2	1834	Ballylagan	Quebec	P
KNOX, Eagleson	26	1834	Ballymaclevennon	Quebec	P
MORISSON, Archibald	33	1833	Ballymaclevennon	Philadelphia	P
MILLER, Elizabeth	18	1833	Crossreagh	Philadelphia	P
MILLER, Alexander	28	1833	Crossreagh	Philadelphia	P
GLENN, William	30	1833	Crossreagh	Philadelphia	P
McHENRY, John	24	1834	Inchmearing	Philadelphia	P
McHENRY, Jane	55	1834	Inchmearing	Philadelphia	P
McSHANE, John	50	1834	Islandmore Upper	Quebec	P
McSHANE, Hester	50	1834	Islandmore Upper	Quebec	P
McSHANE, Eliza Jane	18	1834	Islandmore Upper	Quebec	P
McSHANE, Margaret	13	1834	Islandmore Upeer	Quebec	P
McSHANE, John Jun	6	1834	Islandmore Upper	Quebec	P
McSHANE, Hester Jun	10	1834	Islandmore Upper	Quebec	P
McSHANE, Martha	3	1834	Islandmore Upper	Quebec	P
BLACK, Samuel	60	1834	Glenmanus	New York	P
BLACK, Matilda	36	1833	Glenmanus	New York	P
BLACK, Ellen	28	1833	Glenmanus	New York	P
BLACK, Sarah	35	1833	Glenmanus	New York	P
KING, Susan	35	1833	Magheramenagh	Quebec	P
GASTON, Robert	27	1834	Magheramenagh	Quebec	P
GASTON, Hugh	26	1834	Magheramenagh	Quebec	P
BURNETT, Sinclair	20	1834	Cloyfin North	Philadelphia	P
McMULLAN, Margaret	24	1834	Cloyfin North	Philadelphia	P
WEIR, Hugh	30	1834	Slimag	Philadelphia	P
WIER, Rebeca	34	1833	Slimag	Philadelphia	P
WIER, Margaret Ann	6	1833	Slimag	Philadelphia	P

ORDNANCE SURVEY MEMOIRS

COUNTY: LONDONDERRY
PARISH: BALTEAGH

NAME	AGE	YEAR LEFT	TOWNLAND	DESTINATION	RELI-GION
GEORGE, Alexander	21	1833	Terrydremont North	Philadelphia	P
THOMPSON,Sally	30	1833	Terrydremont North	Philadelphia	P
EAKEN, Alexander	26	1834	Terrydremont North	Philadelphia	P
McMANUS, Mary	20	1833	Terrydremont North	Philadelphia	P
McMANUS, Catherine	18	1834	Terrydremont North	Philadelphia	P
DIAMOND, Mary Ann	6	1834	Terrydremont North	Philadelphia	P
DIAMOND, John	4	1834	Terrydremont North	Philadelphia	P
McCOOL, Joseph	21	1834	Terrydremont North	Philadelphia	P
McGOWEN, Henery	22	1834	Ballyquin	St John	RC
LAFFERTY, Thomas	18	1834	Ballyquin	St John	RC
SMITH, Joseph	18	1833	Carnet	New York	P
LYNN, Ann) Twins	16	1833	Little Derry	New York	P
LYNN, Jane) Twins	16	1833	Little Derry	New York	P
SCULLION, James	18	1833	Ardmore	Quebec	RC
McNAMARA, William	20	1833	Ardmore	Quebec	EC
CEALEY, James	20	1833	Ardmore	Philadelphia	P
ADAMS, Margret	23	1834	Edenmore	New York	P
BOYLE, Elenor	30	1833	Ballymully	New York	RC
BOYLE, Susanna) Twins	1	1833	Ballymully	New York	RC
BOYLE, Sally) Twins	1	1833	Ballymully	New York	RC
BOYLE, Mary Ann	4	1833	Ballymully	New York	RC
BOYLE, John	7	1833	Ballymully	New York	RC
BOYLE, Joseph	5	1833	Ballymully	New York	RC
WOODS, John	20	1834	Drumgosker	Quebec	EC
HUTCHINSON, Robert	22	1834	Lislane	Philadelphia	P
ROSS, David	24	1834	Lislane	Philadelphia	P
ROSS, Jane	26	1834	Lislane	Philadelphia	P
CUNNINGHAM, James	19	1834	Lislane	New York	P
O'KANE, Michael	50	1834	Lislane	New York	RC
O'KANE, Jane	48	1834	Lislane	New York	RC
McCAULEY, Robert	30	1834	Ballyleagry	Philadelphia	P
COLWELL, Thomas	30	1833	Cloghan	Quebec	P
COLWELL, Eliza	32	1833	Cloghan	Quebec	P
McCLOSKEY, John	25	1834	Cloghan	Quebec	RC
McCLOSKEY, Eliza	20	1834	Cloghan	Quebec	RC
BRADLEY, Ann	22	1834	Cloghan	Quebec	RC
BRADLEY, Mary	18	1834	Cloghan	Quebec	RC
McDAID, Patrick	30	1833	Cloghan	Quebec	RC
McDAID, Sally	20	1833	Cloghan	Quebec	RC
MULLEN, Edward	25	1834	Maine	Quebec	P
LAGAN, Mary	20	1834	Drumsurn	Quebec	RCA
LONG, John	18	1834	Drumsurn	Quebec	P
ROSS, David	24	1834	Gortnarney	Philadelphia	P
SCOTT, John	30	1833	Aghansillagh	Philadelphia	P
SCOTT, Robert	32	1834	Aghansillagh	Philadelphia	P
CLYDE, John	21	1833	Terrydoo Clyde	Philadelphia	P
DOONS, John	22	1834	Terrydoo Walker	New York	P
McCAUSLAND, Robert	20	1833	Terrydoo Walker	New York	P
KENEDY, Joseph	30	1834	Ballyavelin	Philadelphia	P
OLLOVER, Bell	18	1833	Drumgesh	Philadelphia	P
OLLOVER, Eliza	20	1833	Drumgesh	Philadelphia	P
LAGAN, Mary	20	1834	Kilhoyle	St John	RC
LOGUE, John	18	1834	Kilhoyle	St John	RC
LOGUE, Bernard	15	1834	Kilhoyle	St John	RC

68

COUNTY: LONDONDERRY

PARISH: BOVEVAGH

NAME	AGE	YEAR LEFT	TOWNLAND	DESTINATION	RELI-GION
McCLENAGHAN, William	17	1833	Drumadreen	New York	RC
SMITH, Alexander	18	1833	Drumadreen	New York	P
DALE, William	40	1833	Drumadreen	New York	P
DALE, Eliza	38	1833	Drumadreen	New York	P
DALE, John	5	1833	Drumadreen	New York	P
LOWDEN, James	40	1834	Drumneechy	Philadelphia	P
LOWDEN, Jane	36	1834	Drumneechy	Philadelphia	P
LOWDEN, Mary	3	1834	Drumneechy	Philadelphia	P
LOWDEN, John	1	1834	Drumneechy	Philadelphia	P
BEGLEY, Neill	20	1833	Drumaduff	Philadelphia	RC
STERLING, Jane	50	1833	Gortaclare	New York	P
STERLING, Ann	25	1833	Gortaclare	New York	P
STERLING, Sally	20	1833	Gortaclare	New York	P
HAMILTON, Joseph	40	1833	Gortaclare	New York	P
HAMILTON, Ann	38	1833	Gortaclare	New York	P
HARAN, Daniel	20	1834	Inisconagher	Quebec	RC
McBETH, James	25	1834	Camnish	Quebec	RC
DOGHERTY, Marcus	18	1833	Camnish	Quebec	RC
BOYLE, John	24	1833	Derrynaflaw	New York	EC
FERGUSON, John	23	1834	Derrynaflaw	New York	P
McCLOSKEY, Patrick	18	1833	Derrynaflaw	Quebec	RC
McCULLY, Andrew	50	1834	Derrynaflaw	Philadelphia	P
McCULLY, Catherine	48	1834	Derrynaflaw	Philadelphia	P
ANDERSON, Alexander	26	1834	Ballymoney	New York	P
FARRIL, Patrick	23	1833	Ballymoney	New York	RC
McCLOSKEY, James	25	1833	Farkland	New York	RC
McCLOSKEY, Eliza	30	1833	Farkland	New York	RC
McLAUGHLIN, Bernard	30	1833	Muldonagh	New York	RC
DEEHAN, Michael	30	1833	Muldonagh	New York	RC
BRAWLEY, Patrick	32	1833	Muldonagh	New York	RC
DEEHAN, Neill	24	1833	Muldonagh	New York	RC
HASSON, Henery	24	1833	Muldonagh	New York	RC
HASSON, Ann	22	1833	Muldonagh	New York	RC
DEEHAN, Mary	20	1833	Muldonagh	New York	RC
DOGHERTY, Ann	20	1833	Muldonagh	New York	RC
McFEELEY, James	35	1833	Muldonagh	New York	RC
McFEELEY, Bernard	20	1834	Muldonagh	New York	RC
McFEELEY, James	40	1833	Muldonagh	New York	RC
HUTTON, James	32	1833	Ballyharigan	St John	P
McCLOSKEY, Margaret	14	1833	Drum	New York	RC
STENSON, John	20	1834	Glenconway	Philadelphia	P
REA, John	20	1834	Glenconway	Philadelphia	P
NUTT, Alexander	18	1834	Glenconway	Philadelphia	P
McCLOSKEY, Grace	25	1833	Gortnahey Beg	Quebec	RC
O'NEILL, James	18	1834	Derrylane	St John	RC
COUGHLIN, Ann	26	1834	Derrylane	St John	RC
BOYLE, Bell	20	1834	Derrylane	St John	P
DONNALDSON, William	20	1834	Flanders	New York	P
HEANEY, Ann	22	1833	Derryyard	Quebec	RC
McENTIRE, John	20	1833	Derryyard	Quebec	RC
McENTIRE, Jane	6	1833	Derryyard	Quebec	RC
McCAY, Mary	20	1833	Derryyard	Quebec	RC
McCAY, Ann	18	1834	Derryyard	Quebec	RC
GUY, Letitia	30	1834	Leeke	New York	P
HAMILTON, Samuel	20	1833	Leeke	Quebec	P
GUY, Maryann	20	1834	Leeke	Quebec	P
DEVLIN, Mary	40	1834	Leeke	Quebec	RC
DEVLIN, Margret	35	1834	Leeke	Quebec	RC
CONNOR, Eliza	48	1834	Leeke	Quebec	EC
McENTIRE, Alexander	18	1833	Leeke	Quebec	P
CONNOR, Margret	20	1834	Leeke	Quebec	EC
DEVLIN, Dennis	40	1834	Leeke	Quebec	RC
DEVLIN, Peter	42	1834	Leeke	Quebec	RC
DEVLIN, James	30	1834	Leeke	Quebec	RC

ORDNANCE SURVEY MEMOIRS

COUNTY: LONDONDERRY
PARISH: BOVEVAGH

NAME	AGE	YEAR LEFT	TOWNLAND	DESTINATION	RELI- GION
DEVLIN, Dennis	26	1834	Leeke	Quebec	RC
DEVLIN, Ann	28	1834	Leeke	Quebec	RC
DEVLIN, Molly	64	1834	Leeke	Quebec	RC
MOORE, John	20	1833	Killybluight	Philadelphia	P
McFADDEN, Samuel	22	1833	Bovevagh	Quebec	P
TAILOR, Robert	20	1833	Bovevagh	Quebec	P
O'KANE, William	24	1834	Bovevagh	Quebec	P
O'KANE, Margret	22	1834	Bovevagh	Quebec	P
QUIGLEY, Kyle	20	1833	Bovevagh	Quebec	EC
MEEHAN, Gordon	20	1834	Bovevagh	Quebec	P
McMANIMEN, James	30	1833	Bovevagh	Quebec	RC
O'KANE, Bryan	28	1833	Ardinarive	Quebec	RC
McCLOSKEY, Elenor	22	1833	Ardinarive	Quebec	RC
McCLOSKEY, Maryann	20	1833	Ardinarive	Quebec	RC
CRAFORD, James	18	1833	Ardinarive	New York	P
DOUGLAS, James	18	1833	Ardinarive	New York	P
STEWART, Robert	20	1833	Templemoyle	New York	P
FORREST, Thomas	25	1833	Templemoyle	Quebec	P
FORREST, John	46	1833	Carrick	New York	P
MULLEN, John	30	1833	Formil	New York	RC

COUNTY: LONDONDERRY

PARISH: COLERAINE

NAME	AGE	YEAR LEFT	TOWNLAND	DESTINATION	RELT-GION
RANKIN, Hugh	16	1834	Blagh	Philadelphia	P
RANKIN, William	18	1833	Blagh	Philadelphia	P
McATYRE, John	25	1834	Ballysally	St John	P
McKEE, William	19	1834	Ballysally	St John	P
McKEE, Ann	23	1834	Ballysally	St John	P
McCLEAN, John	25	1833	Ballysally	Quebec	P
McCLEAN, Jane	20	1833	Ballysally	Quebec	P
KENNEDY, William	18	1834	Crossglebe	Quebec	P
HANNAH, Martha	52	1833	Dundooan	New York	P
HANNAH, John	29	1833	Dundooan	New York	P
HANNAH, Eliza	24	1833	Dundooan	New York	P
HANNAH, Martha	22	1833	Dundooan	New York	P
HANNAH, Lydia	20	1833	Dundooan	New York	P
HANNAH, Robert	18	1833	Dundooan	New York	P
HANNAH, Mary	16	1833	Dundooan	New York	P
HANNAH, Henry	14	1833	Dundooan	New York	P
DUNLOP, Alexander	22	1833	Spittle Hill	Quebec	P
DUNLOP, James	17	1833	Spittle Hill	Quebec	P
McCLELLAND, John	50	1833	Loguestown	Quebec	P
McCLELLAND, Neal	46	1833	Loguestown	Quebec	P
McCLELLAND, Susan	45	1833	Loguestown	Quebec	P
McCLELLAAND, Rachael	19	1833	Loguestown	Quebec	P
McCLELLAND, Maryanne	21	1833	Loguestown	Quebec	P
McCLELLAND, Neal Jun	17	1833	Loguestown	Quebec	P
McCLELLAND, John Jun	14	1833	Loguestown	Quebec	P
McCLELLAND, James	9	1833	Loguestown	Quebec	P
McCLELLAND, Hugh	14	1833	Loguestown	Quebec	P
McCLELLAND, William	3	1833	Loguestown	Quebec	P
McCLELLAND, Susan Jun	5	1833	Loguestown	Quebec	P
McCLELLAND, John Jun	1	1833	Loguestown	Quebec	P
REILLY, James	21	1833	Millburn	Quebec	EC
LITTLE, William	74	1834	Millburn	Scotland	P
LITTLE, Maryanne	35	1834	Millburn	Scotland	P
LITTLE, Andrew	19	1834	Millburn	Scotland	P
LITTLE, George	17	1834	Millburn	Scotland	P
LITTLE, John	15	1834	Millburn	Scotland	P
LITTLE, William Jun	41	1834	Millburn	Scotland	P
LITTLE, Hendrick	9	1834	Millburn	Scotland	P
LITTLE, Maryanne	6	1834	Millburn	Scotland	P
PARKHILL, James	14	1834	Millburn	Scotland	P
KEILLY, William	30	1834	Millburn	Quebec	P
WESTLEY, John	24	1834	Tullans	Philadelphia	P
WILSON, Hester	35	1834	Tullans	New York	P
PARKE, John	35	1833	Tullans	Quebec	P
PARKE, Hannah	28	1833	Tullans	Quebec	P
McCANN, George	21	1833	Tullans	Quebec	RC
STEEL, William	25	1833	Tullans	Quebec	P
BOYD, Henry	40	1833	Tullans	Philadelphia	P
MILLER, John	21	1834	Tullans	Philadelphia	P
MILLER, Margaret	18	1834	Tullans	Philadelphia	P
SHEIL, Thomas	30	1833	Tullans	Philadelphia	P
BROOK, Hugh	28	1834	Tullans	Quebec	P
STEEL, Mary	24	1834	Tullans	Quebec	P
BROOK, Catherine	24	1834	Windy Hall	Quebec	P
McKEE, Alexander	38	1833	Knockantern	Quebec	P
McKEE, Jane	30	1833	Knockantern	Quebec	P
McKEE, William	12	1833	Knockantern	Quebec	P
McKEE, James	10	1833	Knockantern	Quebec	P
McKEE, Margaret Jane	8	1833	Knockantern	Quebec	P
McKEE, Alexander Jun	5	1833	Knockantern	Quebec	P
USHER, John	20	1833	Knockantern	Quebec	P
LYONS, John	25	1833	Knockantern	Quebec	P
McALISTER, Hugh	26	1834	Boghill	Philadelphia	P

ORDNANCE SURVEY MEMOIRS

COUNTY: LONDONDERRY

PARISH: COLERAINE

NAME	AGE	YEAR LEFT	TOWNLAND	DESTINATION	RELI-GION
WRIGHT, James	24	1833	Boghill	Philadelphia	P
GIVEN, Robert	20	1833	Spittle Hill	New York	EC
HEGERTY, Thomas	21	1834	Danes Hill	New York	P
CAULFIELD, Henry	16	1834	Bridge Street	New Orleans	P
McCAY, Samuel	16	1834	Bridge Street	New Orleans	P
GILMOUR, James	19	1834	Bridge Street	New York	P
ORR, William	20	1834	Bridge Street	Quebec	P
KANE, John	35	1834	Diamond	Quebec	P
STEEN, John	50	1834	North Brook St	New York	EC
STEEN, Isabella	48	1834	North Brook St	New York	EC
STEEN, William	18	1834	North Brook St	New York	EC
STEEN, Samuel	7	1834	North Brook St	New York	EC
STEEN, Anne	20	1834	North Brook St	New York	EC
STEEN, Isabel Jun	9	1834	North Brook St	New York	EC
GANNON, Patrick	17	1834	North Brook St	Quebec	RC
McCLEAN, Anne	38	1834	North Brook St	Quebec	P
McCLEAN, James	7	1834	North Brook St	Quebec	P
McCLEAN, John	5	1834	North Brook St	Quebec	P
McCLEAN, Anne	2	1834	North Brook St	Quebec	P
RAMSAY, Samuel	38	1833	New Row	St John	P
RAMSAY, Jane	22	1833	New Row	St John	P
RAMSAY, Catherine	7	1833	New Row	St John	P
RAMSAY, John Jun	5	1833	New Row	St John	P
RAMSAY, Eliza	1mth	1833	New Row	St John	P
RAMSAY, Samuel	3	1833	New Row	St John	P
DUFFY, Thomas	21	1834	New Row	Quebec	RC
MAGROTTY, John	21	1834	New Row	Quebec	RC
DUNLAP, John	24	1834	Blind Gate St	Quebec	EC
HURLEY, Mary	19	1834	Ferry Quay St	Philadelphia	RC
TAYLOR, William	24	1833	Millbrook St	Quebec	EC
TAYLOR, Mary	20	1833	Millbrook St	Quebec	EC
TAYLOR, William	18mths	1833	Millbrook St	Quebec	EC
DOUGLAS, Andrew	22	1833	Mill Brook St	Quebec	EC
MILLER, John	21	1834	Church Street	Philadelphia	P
McCAULEY, Margaret	20	1834	Church Street	New York	P
LINIGAN, Dorathie	23	1834	Diamond	Quebec	P
BLACK, Sibby	45	1833	Blind Gate Street	St John	S
BLACK, James	17	1833	Blind Gate Street	St John	S
BLACK, Mary Anne	4	1833	Blind Gate Street	St John	S
BLACK, Matty	1½	1833	Blind Gate Street	St John	S
BLACK, Eliza	3	1833	Blind Gate Street	St John	S
BLACK, Stewart	14	1833	Blind Gate Street	St John	S
BLACK, Joseph	10	1833	Blind Gate Street	St John	S
BLACK, Robert	3	1833	Blind Gate Street	St John	S
HILL, Archibald	30	1833	Long Commons	St John	P
HILL, Margaret	31	1833	Long Commons	St John	P
HUGHES, John	25	1834	Gaol Lane	New York	P
McLAUGHLIN, Thomas	21	1834	Gaol Lane	New York	RC
CASSIDY, James	24	1834	Gaol Lane	Quebec	RC
McLAUGHLIN, Henry	27	1834	Gaol Lane	New York	RC
SHIELDS, Thomas	24	1834	Ferry Quay Street	New York	M
HUGHES, John	22	1834	Ferry Quay Street	New York	M
McLAUGHLIN, William	35	1834	New Row	Van Dieman's Land	EC
McLAUGHLIN, Hector	20	1834	New Row	Van Dieman's Land	EC
McLAUGHLIN, Charles	20	1834	New Row	Van Dieman's Land	EC
BELL, Thomas	36	1834	Long Commons	Liverpool	P
McLAUGHLIN, Charles	10	1834	Bell House Lane	Van Dieman's Land	P
McINTYRE, John	10	1834	Bell House Lane	Van Dieman's Land	P
BAXTER, William	28	1833	Preaching House Lane	Quebec	EC
RODGERS, James	23	1833	Preaching House Lane	Quebec	EC
HINDS, John	40	1834	Society School House	London	P
HINDS, Hariot	40	1834	Society School House	London	P
HINDS, John Jun	12	1834	Society School House	London	P
HINDS, Hariot	10	1834	Society School House	London	P

COUNTY: LONDONDERRY

PARISH: COLERAINE

NAME	AGE	YEAR LEFT	TOWNLAND	DESTINATION	RELI-GION
HINDS, Mary	9	1834	Society School House	London	P
HINDS, William	8	1834	Society School House	London	P
HINDS, Frederick	6	1834	Society School House	London	P
HINDS, Charles	5	1834	Society School House	London	P
HINDS, James	4	1834	Society School House	London	P
HINDS, Arthur	2	1834	Society School House	London	P
McINTYRE, John	50	1834	Shamble Street	Quebec	S
CREIGHTON, William	25	1834	Society Street	New York	P
CREIGHTON, Elizabeth	30	1834	Society Street	New York	P
WILLIAMSON, Charles	25	1833	Rampart	Quebec	P
WILLIAMSON, Margaret	30	1833	Rampart	Quebec	P
WILLIAMSON, James	1	1833	Rampart	Quebec	P

ORDNANCE SURVEY MEMOIRS

COUNTY: LONDONDERRY
PARISH: DESERTOGHILL

NAME	AGE	YEAR LEFT	TOWNLAND	DESTINATION	RELI-GION
WATT, John	25	1833	Ballynameen	Quebec	P
WATT, Maryann	23	1833	Ballynameen	Quebec	P
McINTOSH, William	20	1833	Ballynameen	Quebec	P
HOLMES, Joseph	28	1833	Ballynameen	New York	P
TRACY, James	18	1833	Carrowreagh	Quebec	RC
TRACY, Joseph	20	1833	Carrowreagh	Quebec	RC
QUIGG, James	26	1833	Carrowreagh	Quebec	RC
QUIGG, Jane	30	1833	Carrowreagh	Quebec	RC
SHUTTER, David	40	1833	Carballintober	Quebec	P
SHUTTER, Margaret	40	1833	Carballintober	Quebec	P
SHUTTER, George	16	1833	Carballintober	Quebec	P
SHUTTER, Elizabeth	14	1833	Carballintober	Quebec	P
SHUTTER, William	12	1833	Carballintober	Quebec	P
SHUTTER, Martha	8	1833	Carballintober	Quebec	P
SHUTTER, David Jun.	2	1833	Carballintober	Quebec	P
SHUTTER, Margaret Jun.	5	1833	Carballintober	Quebec	P
WADE, Thomas	30	1833	Carballintober	Quebec	P
HAMPSEY, Elizabeth	24	1833	Cuilbane	St John	RC
SMITH, James	30	1833	Coolymann	Glasgow	P
SMITH, John	27	1833	Coolymann	Glasgow	P
MORRILL, Samuel	26	1833	Coolymann	Glasgow	P
McDAID, Daniel	40	1833	Coolymann	Glasgow	RC
McDAID, Sarah	30	1833	Coolymann	Glasgow	RC
McDAID, Maryanne	1	1833	Coolymann	Glasgow	RC
McDAID, Sarah Jun.	7	1833	Coolymann	Glasgow	RC
McDAID, Margaret	5	1833	Coolymann	Glasgow	RC
KANE, James	26	1833	Coolbane	Liverpool	RC
McNICOLLS, Daniel	24	1833	Coolbane	Liverpool	RC
NEIL, John	20	1833	Coolbane	Liverpool	RC
NEIL, HUGH	27	1833	Coolbane	Liverpool	RC
HAMPSEY, Patrick	25	1833	Coolbane	Liverpool	RC
HAMPSEY, Jane	22	1833	Coolbane	Liverpool	RC
MULHOLLAND, Andrew	23	1833	Coolbane	Liverpool	RC
MULHOLLAND, Hugh	20	1833	Coolbane	Liverpool	RC
BOWTON, Hugh	21	1833	Dullaghy	New York	P
MAHARG, John	25	1833	Gortycloghan	Quebec	P
YOUNG, Hugh	30	1833	Gortycloghan	Quebec	P
MAHARG, Sarah	22	1833	Gortycloghan	Quebec	P
MAHARG, Robert	3	1833	Gortycloghan	Quebec	P
MAHARG, Mary	3mths	1833	Gortycloghan	Quebec	P
NICOLLS, Robert	24	1833	Killyvally	New York	P
NICOLLS, Sarah	34	1833	Killyvally	New York	P
McINTOSH, William	18	1833	Killyvally	Philadelphia	P
McKOOK, Rebecca	30	1833	Kurin	Quebec	P
THOMSON, David	23	1833	Moylitra Kill	Quebec	P
McALISTER, Jonathan	24	1833	Moylitra Kill	Quebec	P
McALISTER, William	30	1833	Moylitra Kill	Quebec	P
McCLERY, William	40	1833	Moylitra Toy	Quebec	EC
McCLERY, Mary	35	1833	Moylitra Toy	Quebec	EC
McCLERY, William	10	1833	Moylitra Toy	Quebec	EC
McCLERY, Ellen	8	1833	Moylitra Toy	Quebec	EC
FAITH, Mary	25	1833	Moylitra Toy	Quebec	EC
DOGHERTY, Robert	24	1833	Maghgramore	St John	P
BELL, Joseph	32	1833	Movenis	Quebec	P
BELL, Margaret	21	1833	Movenis	Quebec	P
ELDER, Henry	18	1834	Ballury	Quebec	P
NICOLLS, James	21	1834	Ballyagan	Quebec	P
SMITH, James	25	1834	Ballyagan	St John	P
NICOLLS, Thomas	24	1834	Ballyagan	New York	P
BOYD, Jane	35	1834	Coolymann	New York	P
BOYD, Jane Jun.	13	1834	Coolymann	New York	P
BOYD, Margaret	11	1834	Coolymann	New York	P
BOYD, Elizabeth	9	1834	Coolymann	New York	P
BOYD, Cornelius	7	1834	Coolymann	New York	P

ORDNANCE SURVEY MEMOIRS

COUNTY: LONDONDERRY
PARISH: DESERTOGHILL

NAME	AGE	YEAR LEFT	TOWNLAND	DESTINATION	RELI-GION
BOYD, Mary	5	1834	Coolymann	New York	P
LINTON, Archibald	42	1834	Coolymann	New York	P
LINTON, Catherine	38	1834	Coolymann	Quebec	P
LINTON, Margaret	18	1834	Coolymann	Quebec	P
LINTON, Thomas	16	1834	Coolymann	Quebec	P
LINTON, James	14	1834	Coolymann	Quebec	P
LINTON, Martha	12	1834	Coolymann	Quebec	P
LINTON, Catherine Jun.	10	1834	Coolymann	Quebec	P
LINTON, Joseph	8	1834	Coolymann	Quebec	P
LINTON, Anne	4	1834	Coolymann	Quebec	P
GRIBBEN, James	18	1834	Crossland	Quebec	RC
McKAGUE, James	20	1834	Crossland	Glasgow	RC
McKAGUE, Charles	26	1834	Crossland	Glasgow	RC
WALLACE, Alexander	35	1834	Dullaghy	Quebec	P
WALLACE, Anne	32	1834	Dullaghy	Quebec	P
MAHARG, William	30	1834	Gortycloghan	St John	P
DOHERTY, Robert	30	1834	Gortycloghan	St John	P
KENNEDY, Robert	30	1834	Gortycloghan	St John	P
McCOOK, James	44	1834	Movenis	Quebec	P
McCOOK, Jane	40	1834	Movenis	Quebec	P
McCOOK, John	16	1834	Movenis	Quebec	P
McCOOK, Mary Jane	18	1834	Movenis	Quebec	P
McCOOK, Eliza	20	1834	Movenis	Quebec	P
McCOOK, Martha	12	1834	Movenis	Quebec	P
McCOOK, Rebecca	30	1834	Movenis	Quebec	P
McDAID, Cornelius	55	1834	Movenis	Quebec	P
McDAID, Mary	42	1834	Movenis	Quebec	P
McDAID, Jane	20	1834	Movenis	Quebec	P
McDAID, John	15	1834	Movenis	Quebec	P
BRADLEY, Hugh	25	1834	Magheramore	Liverpool	P
TOIGHIL, Anthony	28	1834	Magheramore	Liverpool	P
McCAHEY, James	50	1834	Moyletra Toy	New York	P
McCAHEY, John	30	1834	Moyletra Toy	New York	P
SHEDIN, Captain	50	1834	Moyletra Toy	Quebec	EC
SHEDIN, Mary	45	1834	Moyletra Toy	Quebec	EC
SHEDIN, William	6	1834	Moyletra Toy	Quebec	EC
SHEDIN, John	5	1834	Moyletra Toy	Quebec	EC
SHEDIN, Eliza	4	1834	Moyletra Toy	Quebec	EC
SHEDIN, Mary Jun.	3	1834	Moyletra Toy	Quebec	EC
SHEDIN, Thomas	2	1834	Moyletra Toy	Quebec	EC
SHEDIN, James	1	1834	Moyletra Toy	Quebec	EC
DOHERTY, James	35	1834	Moyletra Toy	Quebec	RC
JOHNSTON, John	30	1834	Moyletra Toy	Quebec	RC
BOYLE, James	50	1834	Moyletra Toy	Quebec	RC

COUNTY: LONDONDERRY

PARISH: DRUMACHOSE

NAME	AGE	YEAR LEFT	TOWNLAND	DESTINATION	RELI-GION
McCLOWD, James	30	1833	Drummond	St John	P
GALLAGHER, Patrick	22	1833	Drummond	St John	RC
LYNN, David	20	1833	Drummond	St John	RC
MARTIN, Oliver	40	1833	Drummond	St John	P
MARTIN, Thomas	22	1833	Drummond	St John	P
HAGHERTY, Joseph	28	1833	Drummond	St John	P
McCONAGHY, William	16	1834	Drummond	New York	P
COOK, James	40	1834	Drummond	St John	P
COOK, Jane	38	1834	Drummond	St John	P
COOK, Daniel	20	1833	Drummond	St John	P
COOK, Ann	18	1833	Drummond	St John	P
COOK, Jane	14	1833	Drummond	St John	P
COOK, Kittyann	8	1834	Drummond	St John	P
COOK, Bell	10	1834	Drummond	St John	P
COOK, James	6	1834	Drummond	St John	P
MULLIN, Molly	30	1834	Drummond	St John	RC
MULLIN, Marcus	10	1834	Drummond	St John	RC
MULLIN, Edward	6	1834	Drummond	St John	RC
MULLIN, Patrick	4	1834	Drummond	St John	RC
MULLIN, Robert	2	1834	Drummond	St John	RC
MULLIN, John	8	1834	Drummond	St John	RC
GREY, Elenor	30	1834	Drummond	St John	RC
McCAY, Mary	26	1834	Drummond	St John	RC
BRAWLEY, John	24	1834	Drummond	St John	RC
McMACKEN, John	22	1834	Drummond	St John	RC
DOGHERTY, James	17	1834	Drummond	Philadelphia	RC
MULLIN, Docia	22	1833	Drummond	St John	RC
CONWAY, William	10	1833	Drummond	St John	RC
RIGHT, Hugh	64	1834	Bovally	St John	P
CONNOR, William	24	1833	Ardgarvan	St John	RC
BROWN, William	30	1833	Rathbrady Beg	Philadelphia	P
McCLARY, Hugh	22	1833	Rathbrady Beg	New York	EC
McALLISTER, Robert	18	1833	Rathbrady Beg	St John	EC
TAGGART, John	26	1833	Rathbrady Beg	New York	RC
TAGGART, Patrick	16	1833	Rathbrady Beg	New York	RC
SCOTT, James	24	1833	Rathbrady Beg	Quebec	EC
GREER, William	24	1833	Rathbrady Beg	St John	EC
FLANIGAN, James	28	1834	Rathbrady Beg	Quebec	EC
FLANIGAN, Eliza	26	1834	Rathbrady Beg	Quebec	EC
FLANIGAN, Allice	4	1834	Rathbrady Beg	Quebec	EC
MILLIN, Maryanne	18	1834	Rathbrady Beg	Quebec	P
McFAULL, Daniel	23	1834	Rathbrady Beg	St John	EC
McLAUGHLIN, Patrick	26	1834	Rathbrady Beg	St John	RC
McLAUGHLIN, Maryanne	24	1834	Rathbrady Beg	St John	RC
McLAUGHLIN, William	18	1834	Rathbrady Beg	St John	RC
McLAUGHLIN, James	30	1834	Rathbrady Beg	St John	RC
McELVAN, John	19	1834	Rathbrady Beg	St John	RC
LYNN, David	19	1834	Rathbrady Beg	St John	RC
HUNTER, William	23	1833	Rathbrady Beg	Quebec	P
CALLAGHAN, Joseph	20	1833	Rathbrady Beg	Van Dieman's Land	P
CALLAGHAN, James	20	1833	Rathbrady Beg	New South Wales	EC
NODWELL, Mathew	30	1834	Glenkeen	St John	P
NODWELL, Catherine	28	1834	Glenkeen	St John	P
NODWELL, Maryann	5	1834	Glenkeen	St John	P
NODWELL, Eliza	3	1834	Glenkeen	St John	P
RANKIN, Thomas	30	1834	Tirmaquin	New York	P
JOHNSTON, John	18	1833	Tirmaquin	Philadelphia	P
HENERY, Molly	40	1833	Tirmaquin	Philadelphia	P
KENEDY, Rachael	50	1833	Tirmaquin	Philadelphia	P
KENEDY, Joseph	30	1834	Ballyavelin	Philadelphia	P
KENEDY, Jane	28	1834	Ballyavelin	Philadelphia	P
KENEDY, Mary	10	1834	Ballyavelin	Philadelphia	P
KENEDY, Martha	7	1834	Ballyavelin	Philadelphia	P
KENEDY, George	5	1834	Ballyavelin	Philadelphia	P

COUNTY: LONDONDERRY
PARISH: DRUMACHOSE

NAME	AGE	YEAR LEFT	TOWNLAND	DESTINATION	RELI-GION
KENEDY. Fullerton	3	1834	Ballyavelin	Philadelphia	P
KENEDY, (Male)	1	1834	Ballyavelin	Philadelphia	P
GARVEN, Patrick	20	1833	Drumramer	St John	RC
McSPARREN, Archibald	40	1833	Drumramer	Philadelphia	P
McSPARREN, Miss	35	1833	Drumramer	Philadelphia	P
RICHY, James	50	1833	Ballycrum	St John	P
RICHY, Molly	48	1833	Ballycrum	St John	P
RICHY, Samuel	20	1833	Ballycrum	St John	P
RICHY, James	18	1833	Ballycrum	St John	P
DOUGLAS, George	20	1833	Leck	St John	P
DOUGLAS, Margaret	21	1833	Leck	St John	P
CANNING, John	20	1834	Largyreagh	Philadelphia	P
CANNING, Marcus	18	1834	Largyreagh	Philadelphia	P
CANNING, Annjane	11	1834	Largyreagh	Philadelphia	P
STERLING, Matilda	22	1834	Largyreagh	Philadelphia	P
CONN, John	25	1833	Gortgarn	New York	P
FLANIGAN, John	1	1834	Newtown Limavady or Rathbrady Beg	Quebec	EC
FLANIGAN, Maryann	3	1834	Newtown Limavady or Rathbrady Beg	Quebec	EC
DOGHERTY, Conoley	18	1833	Newtown Limavady or Rathbrady Beg	New York	RC
GIVEN, William	18	1833	Newtown Limavady or Rathbrady Beg	New York	EC
McLAUGHLIN, James	24	1833	Newtown Limavady or Rathbrady Beg	New York	RC
McLAUGHLIN, Catherine	18	1833	Newtown Limavady or Rathbrady Beg	New York	RC
MURRAY, Elenor	35	1834	Newtown Limavady or Rathbrady Beg	New York	RC
MURRAY, Maryann	15	1834	Newtown Limavady or Rathbrady Beg	New York	RC
MURRAY, Edward	46	1833	Newtown Limavady or Rathbrady Beg	New York	RC
MURRAY, Daniel	18	1833	Newtown Limavady or Rathbrady Beg	New York	RC
MURRAY, Edward	17	1833	Newtown Limavady or Rathbrady Beg	New York	RC
HUNTER, William	24	1834	Rathbrady More	New York	P
MULLEN, Edward	24	1834	Derrybeg	New York	P
LINSEY, Sarah	20	1834	Derrmore	Philadelphia	P
LINSEY, Eliza	18	1834	Derrmore	Philadelphia	P
LINSEY, James	20	1834	Derrmore	Philadelphia	P
McCLOSKEY, James	26	1833	Bolea	Philadelphia	P
SMITH, Samual	20	1833	Bolea	Philadelphia	P
CAMPBELL, William	20	1833	Bolea	Philadelphia	P
McCLOSKEY, Jane	28	1833	Bolea	Philadelphia	P
WISELY, Martin	18	1833	Bolea	Philadelphia	P
WISELY, Margaret	45	1834	Bolea	Philadelphia	P
WISELY, William	16	1834	Bolea	Philadelphia	P
MULLEN, Charles	24	1834	Dunbeg	Philadelphia	RC
ALLEN, George	26	1833	Ballyriskmore	Philadelphia	P
McFEETRIDGE, Robert	28	1833	Ballyriskmore	Philadelphia	P
LOUGRY, Michael	26	1833	Coolessan	Quebec	RC
EATON, Mary	22	1833	Coolessan	Quebec	RC

COUNTY: LONDONDERRY

PARISH: DUNBOE

NAME	AGE	YEAR LEFT	TOWNLAND	DESTINATION	RELI- GION
DONAHY, Nancy	25	1833	Articlave	St John	P
McGAUNEY, Francis	30	1833	Articlave	St John	EC
McGAUNEY, James	22	1833	Articlave	St John	EC
SMITH, Mary	22	1833	Articlave	Quebec	P
SMITH, Robert	4mths	1833	Articlave	Quebec	P
COLEMAN, Cochran	18	1833	Articlave	St John	EC
COLEMAN, Mary	30	1833	Articlave	St John	EC
THORPE, Stephen	18	1833	Articlave	St John	EC
PAUL, William	50	1833	Atriclave	St John	P
PAUL, Sarah	16	1833	Articlave	St John	P
PAUL, Elizabeth	45	1833	Alticlave	St John	P
BROSTER, Alexander	40	1833	Knocknogher	Philadelphia	P
STERLING, Cochran	28	1833	Knockmult	St John	P
SMITH, Gilbert	22	1833	Bennarees	Quebec	P
SMITH, Elizabeth	22	1833	Bennarees	Quebec	P
FULGRAVE, Robert	24	1833	Fermoyle	St John	P
BLACK, Ellen	22	1833	Fermoyle	Quebec	P
LESTLY, George	30	1833	Bratwell	Philadelphia	P
CLARKE, John	21	1833	Bratwell	Quebec	P
CLARKE, Nancy	30	1833	Bratwell	Quebec	P
CLARKE, Jane	2	1833	Bratwell	Quebec	P
ROSS, Mary	22	1833	Sconce	Quebec	P
ROSS, Margaret	22	1833	Sconce	Quebec	P
ROSS, Thomas	36	1833	Sconce	Quebec	P
ROSS, Jane	24	1833	Sconce	Quebec	P
ROSS, Thomas	36	1833	Sconce	Quebec	P
ROSS, Jane	24	1833	Sconce	Quebec	P
ROSS. Robert Jun	6	1833	Sconce	Quebec	P
ROSS, Thomas	4	1833	Sconce	Quebec	P
McLAUGHLIN, George	32	1833	Mullan Head	Quebec	RC
SMITH, William	22	1833	Fermullan	St John	P
DEVENY, William	20	1833	Farnlester	Quebec (returned 1834)	RC
SMITH, John	22	1833	Ballyhacket Glenahoy	Quebec	P
SMITH, Ellen	32	1833	Ballyhacket Glenahoy	Quebec	P
McLAUGHLIN, John	1	1833	Ballyhacket Glenahoy	Quebec	P
BLAIR, James Sen.	26	1833	Ballywildrick	Philadelphia	P
BLAIR, Mary	20	1833	Ballywildrick	Philadelphia	P
CLARKE, John	20	1833	Ballywoodock	Philadelphia	P
BROSTER, Thomas	20	1833	Glebe	Philadelphia	P
BROSTER, Mary	18	1833	Glebe	Philadelphia	P
BROSTER, Jane	20	1833	Glebe	Philadelphia	P
McMULLEN, Isaac	20	1833	Ardina	Philadelphia	P
HAZLETT, Charles	35	1833	Bogtown	Philadelphia	P
EVANS, Hugh	20	1834	Articlave	St John	P
BEATY, John	28	1834	Articlave	New York	P
RAY, Robert	18	1834	Knocknogher	Philadelphia	P
HINDMAN, Margret	22	1834	Killyveety	Quebec	P
WILSON, Charles	25	1833	Pottagh	Philadelphia	P
BOND, John	32	1834	Bratwell	Philadelphia	P
BOND, Anne	27	1834	Bratwell	Philadelphia	P
BOND, Mary	5	1834	Bratwell	Philadelphia	P
BOND,Margret	2½	1834	Bratwell	Philadelphia	P
BOND, Barbara	2	1834	Bratwell	Philadelphia	P
McLAUGHLIN, John	25	1834	Bellany	Philadelphia	RC
DUNLOP, Jane	23½	1834	Drunagully	New York	RC
JOHNSTON, Thomas	26	1834	Drunagully	St John	RC
McCLEMENT, Robert	19	1834	Drunagully	St John	RC
McLAUGHLIN, William	29	1834	Ballyhacket Glenahoy	Quebec	RC
McLAUGHLIN, Mary	25	1834	Ballyhacket Glenahoy	Quebec	RC
BLAIR, James	22	1834	Ballywildrake	Philadelphia	RC
WARK, Isaac	20	1834	Ballywoodock	Philadelphia	RC
ALEXANDER, John	18	1834	Ballywoodock	Philadelphia	RC
WILLIAMS, James	18	1834	Altibrian	New York	RC

ORDNANCE SURVEY MEMOIRS

COUNTY: LONDONDERRY

PARISH: ERRIGAL

NAME	AGE	YEAR LEFT	TOWNLAND	DESTINATION	RELI-GION
WALKER, William	19	1834	Mettican Glebe	New York	EC
TURBITT, John	28	1833	Cah	Quebec	P
TURBITT, Margrett	21	1833	Cah	Quebec	P
MULLEN, Michael	21	1834	Ballygrogan	Quebec	RC
McCLOSKEY, Michael	22	1834	Ballygrogan	Quebec	RC
HIGGINS, Bernard	23	1833	Ballygrogan	Quebec	RC
McBEATH, Henery	30	1834	Coolnasillagh	Quebec	RC
McBEATH, Margrett	28	1834	Coolnasillagh	Quebec	RC
McBEATH, John	5	1834	Coolnasillagh	Quebec	RC
McBEATH, Magy	3	1834	Coolnasillagh	Quebec	RC
McBEATH, William	1	1834	Coolnasillagh	Quebec	RC
MULLEN, Thomas	35	1834	Frugh	New York	RC
McPHERSON, James	40	1834	Frugh	Philadelphia	RC
CRILLY, Michael	19	1834	Farrentemple	Quebec	RC
MOONEY, John	17	1834	Farrentemple	Quebec	RC
McCLOSKEY, John	25	1833	Ballintemple	St John	RC
McCLOSKEY, Ann	19	1833	Ballintemple	St John	RC
O'KANE, Michael	40	1834	Ballintemple	New York	RC
O'KANE, James	46	1834	Ballintemple	New York	RC
O'KANE, John	22	1834	Ballintemple	New York	RC
O'KANE, James	19	1834	Ballintemple	New York	RC
O'KANE, Patt	17	1834	Ballintemple	New York	RC
O'KANE, Michael	15	1834	Ballintemple	New York	RC
O'KANE, Jane	9	1834	Ballintemple	New York	RC
O'KANE, Cormic	35	1834	Ballintemple	New York	RC
DIAMOND, Patt	23	1834	Gortnamoyagh	New York	RC
MULLEN, John	40	1833	Brockaghboy	Quebec	RC
MULLEN, Mary	35	1833	Brockaghboy	Quebec	RC
MULLEN, Patt	11	1833	Brockaghboy	Quebec	RC
MULLEN, Mary	7	1833	Brockaghboy	Quebec	RC
MULLEN, Ann	5	1833	Brockaghboy	Quebec	RC
MULLEN, Bernard	24	1833	Brockagh	Boston	RC
MULLEN, James	26	1833	Brockagh	Boston	RC
CRAIG, Robert	30	1833	Inishaleen	Philadelphia	P
CRAIG, James	20	1833	Inishaleen	Philadelphia	P
CASSIDY, James	20	1834	Garvagh	Quebec	RC
O'KANE, Ritchard	22	1833	Garvagh	Quebec	RC
McCLOSKEY, Ritchard	18	1833	Garvagh	Quebec	RC
LAMMINS, James	30	1833	Garvagh	Quebec	RC
LAMMINS, Hanna	28	1833	Garvagh	Quebec	RC
MULHOLLAND, Charles	20	1833	Garvagh	Quebec	RC
DOORIS, James	46	1834	Garvagh	Quebec	RC
DOORIS, Mary	30	1834	Garvagh	Quebec	RC
CRILLY, Bernard	30	1834	Garvagh	Quebec	RC
CRILLY, Bridget	25	1834	Garvagh	Quebec	RC
CRILLY, John	3	1834	Garvagh	Quebec	RC
CRILLY, Ann	6mths	1834	Garvagh	Quebec	RC
AUTHORSON, Samual	20	1834	Garvagh	Quebec	RC

COUNTY: LONDONDERRY
PARISH: KILCRONAGHAN

NAME	AGE	YEAR LEFT	TOWNLAND	DESTINATION	RELI-GION
GILMOUR, Jane	23	1834	Tobermore	Quebec	EC
GILMOUR, Nancy	20	1834	Tobermore	Quebec	EC
McKEEVER, Eliza	18	1834	Tobermore	Quebec	EC
WRIGHT, Sarah	21	1834	Tobermore	Quebec	EC
LAIRD, Hannah	22	1834	Tobermore	Quebec	EC
HUGHS, John	34	1834	Moyesset	Quebec	EC
DEVLIN, Anne	20	1834	Killynumber	Quebec	RC
NEELY, Thomas	25	1834	Closfin	Philadelphia	P
CLARKE, Sarah	20	1834	Tamnyaskin	Philadelphia	P
CAMPBELL, Archy	22	1834	Granny	Quebec	P
CAMPBELL, Charles	17	1834	Granny	Quebec	P
CAMPBELL, Robert	25	1834	Granny	Quebec	P
McKEE, William	18	1834	Granny	Philadelphia	P
ESPY, Jane	20	1834	Granny	Philadelphia	P
ESPY, Sarah	22	1834	Granny	Philadelphia	P
ESPY, David	19	1834	Granny	Philadelphia	P
McCARTNEY, James	30	1834	Tullyroan	Philadelphia	RC
HART, Thomas	24	1834	Mormeal	Philadelphia	P
HART, Mary	30	1834	Mormeal	Philadelphia	P
SHEAGOG, William	25	1834	Brackaghrowley	St John	EC
CLARKE, Mathew	45	1834	Drumballyhagan Clark	St John	EC
McKEEVER, Michael	35	1834	Moybeg Kirley	New York	RC
McKEEVER, Margaret	37	1834	Moybeg Kirley	New York	RC
McKEEVER, Maryanne	5	1834	Moybeg Kirley	New York	RC
McKEEVER, Catherine	3	1834	Moybeg Kirley	New York	RC
McKEEVER, John	1	1834	Moybeg Kirley	New York	RC
HIGGINS, James	24	1834	Keenaght	Philadelphia	RC
REGAN, Denis	33	1834	Keenaght	Philadelphia	RC
HIGGINS, Sarah	24	1834	Keenaght	Philadelphia	RC
KEARNEY, Bridget	21	1834	Keenaght	Philadelphia	RC
KEARNEY, John	28	1834	Keenaght	Philadelphia	RC
LYLE, John	35	1834	Tullyroan	Philadelphia	I
McKEE, Henry George	20	1834	Tullyroan	Philadelphia	I
STEWART, William	20	1834	Tullyroan	Philadelphia	I
McWILLIAM, James	19	1834	Mormeal	Philadelphia	RC
McSHANE, John	35	1834	Mormeal	Van Dieman's Land	RC
HENRY, Patrick	22	1834	Mormeal	Van Dieman's Land	RC
STEWART, Mathew	22	1834	Granny	Glasgow	EC
STEWART, Jane	25	1834	Granny	Glasgow	EC
STEWART, Robert	1	1834	Granny	Glasgow	EC
McCART, Sarah	30	1834	Granny	Glasgow	EC
STEWART, Ellen	20	1834	Granny	Glasgow	EC
NEIL, Sarah	30	1834	Drumsamney	Quebec	RC
NEIL, Margaret	28	1834	Drumsamney	Quebec	RC
NEIL, James	17	1834	Drumsamney	Quebec	RC
NEIL, John	19	1834	Drumsamney	Quebec	RC
NEIL, Mary	15	1834	Drumsamney	Quebec	RC

COUNTY: LONDONDERRY

SEASONAL MIGRANTS

PARISH: KILCRONAGHAN

NAME	AGE	YEAR LEFT	TOWNLAND	DESTINATION	RELI-GION
HAGAN, James	20		Brackaghrowley	Merryport	RC
HAGAN, Patrick	30		Brackaghrowley	England	RC
MURPHY, John	22		Brackaghrowley	England	RC
REILLY, Andrew	20		Brackaghrowley	England	RC
KELLY, Patrick	22		Brackaghrowley	England	RC
CARNEY, Patrick	27		Brackaghrowley	England	RC
McNAMEE, Peter	35		Brackaghrowley	England	RC
HAGAN, Michael	30		Brackaghrowley	England	RC
McKEEVER, Michael	25		Brackaghrowley	England	RC
McKEEVER, Frank	35		Brackaghrowley	England	RC
McGUIGAN, Frank	35		Brackaghrowley	England	RC
McGUIGAN, Patrick	25		Brackaghrowley	Englànd	RC
McGUIGAN, Frank	32		Brackaghrowley	England	RC
McGUIGAN, John	30		Brackaghrowley	England	RC
McGUIGAN, Daniel	38		Brackaghlislea	Merryport	RC
MAGOWAN, Frank	21		Brackaghlislea	Merryport	RC
TRAINER, James	27		Brackaghlislea	Merryport	RC
ONEIL, Patrick	22		Brackaghlislea	Merryport	RC
McBRIDE, Edward	23		Brackaghlislea	Merryport	RC
McCRISTAL, Michael	40		Brackaghlislea	Merryport	RC
GALLIGHER, Michael	35		Brackaghlislea	Merryport	RC
KELLY, Patrick	30		Brackaghlislea	Merryport	RC
KELLY, Andrew	32		Brackaghlislea	Merryport	RC
McGUIGAN, James	45		Brackaghlislea	Merryport	RC
HENRY, James	22		Brackaghlislea	Merryport	RC
McCANN, Charles	38		Brackaghlislea	Merryport	RC
McKEEVER, Daniel	35		Gortahurk	Merryport	RC
BRYAN, Henry	25		Gortahurk	Merryport	RC
McWILLIAM, Michael	28		Keenaught	England	RC
BRYAN, James	28		Keenaught	England	RC
BRYAN, Andrew	28		Keenaught	England	RC
HANNAH, James	35		Tobermore	Glasgow	P
DEVLIN, Peter	25		Tobermore	Glasgow	P
CONVEAY, Ambrose	21		Tobermore	Glasgow	P
CALLIGHAN, Frank	30		Tobermore	Glasgow	P
COLGAN, Charles	24		Tobermore	Glasgow	P
STEWART, Andrew	40		Granny	Glasgow	EC
TONER, Hugh	30		Mormeal	Glasgow	RC
CRILLY, James	26		Mormeal	Glasgow	RC
CAMPBELL, William	25		Mormeal	Glasgow	P
BURNSIDE, William	25		Mormeal	Glasgow	P
MELON, John	20		Mormeal	Glasgow	P
McCORT, George	26		Mormeal	Glasgow	EC
TONER, Patrick	50		Mormeal	Glasgow	RC
HARA, Owen	20		Mormeal	Glasgow	RC
STEWART, James	19		Mormeal	Glasgow	EC
DEVINE, John	40		Granny	Glasgow	EC
PEADY, William	30		Tamnyaskey	Glasgow	EC
GIBSON, William	25		Tamnyaskey	Glasgow	I
LYLE, David	36		Tamnyaskey	Glasgow	P
PERRY, William	32		Tamnyaskey	Glasgow	EC
McCALISTER, John	27		Moybegkirley	England	RC
BRYANS, Thomas	20		Culmore	England	P
BRYANS, John	22		Culmore	England	P

ORDNANCE SURVEY MEMOIRS

NAME	AGE	YEAR LEFT	TOWNLAND	DESTINATION	RELI-GION
HUNTER, Daniel	40	1834	Damhead	Quebec	P
HUNTER, Jane	28	1834	Damhead	Quebec	P
NELIS, William	42	1834	Damhead	Quebec	P
NELIS, Andrew	18	1834	Damhead	Quebec	P
MORRISON, David	28	1834	Damhead	Quebec	P
POLLOCK, Robert	20	1834	Coolderry South	Quebec	P
McCARROLL, Hugh	24	1834	Coolderry South	Quebec	P
McCARROLL, Eliza	26	1834	Coolderry South	Quebec	P
McGETTY, Alexander	35	1834	Coolderry South	Philadelphia	P
McGETTY, Martha	40	1834	Coolderry South	Philadelphia	P
McGETTY, Matilda	8	1834	Coolderry South	Philadelphia	P
McGETTY, Margaret	6	1834	Coolderry South	Philadelphia	P
STEEL, Hugh	60	1834	Mill Loughan	Quebec	P
STEEL, Ann	64	1834	Mill Loughan	Quebec	P
STEEL, Samuel	16	1834	Mill Loughan	Quebec	P
STEEL, Mary	22	1834	Mill Loughan	Quebec	P
HEMPHILL, Martha	11	1834	Mill Loughan	Quebec	P
HUNTER, James	72	1834	Loughanreagh South	Quebec	P
HUNTER, Nicholas	68	1834	Loughanreagh South	Quebec	P
HUNTER, William	42	1834	Loughanreagh South	Quebec	P
HUNTER, James	27	1834	Loughanreagh South	Quebec	P
HUNTER, Robert	23	1834	Loughanreagh South	Quebec	P
HUNTER, Margaret	36	1834	Loughanreagh South	Quebec	P
HUNTER, Agnes	19	1834	Loughanreagh South	Quebec	P
HUNTER, Mary	21	1834	Loughanreagh South	Quebec	P

COUNTY: LONDONDERRY
PARISH: KILLOWEN

NAME	AGE	YEAR LEFT	TOWNLAND	DESTINATION	RELIGION
KANE, Maryann	23	1833	Killowen	New York	EC
McGOWEN, Ann	20	1833	Killowen	St John	RC
McGOWEN, James	16	1833	Killowen	St John	RC
HUGHES, John	22	1833	Killowen	New York	EC
YEATES, Mathew	20	1833	Killowen	New York	EC
McDONOUGH, Charles	18	1833	Waterside	Quebec	RC
FARRAN, William	25	1833	Waterside	Quebec	RC
McCORMICK, Henry	20	1833	Waterside	Quebec	RC
COYLE, Patt	35	1833	Waterside	Quebec	RC
COYLE, Sally	33	1833	Waterside	Quebec	RC
McLAUGHLIN, William	20	1833	Waterside	Quebec	RC
GANNON, Richard	30	1833	Waterside	Quebec	RC
WILSON, James	40	1833	Waterside	Quebec	P
MOORE, James	18	1833	Ballycairn	Quebec	RC
MOORE, John	26	1833	Ballycairn	Quebec	RC
MOORE, William	21	1833	Ballycairn	Quebec	RC
MURPHY, Binn	16	1833	Ballycairn	Quebec	EC
GAGE, James	21	1833	Killcranny	Philadelphia	P
McLAUGHLIN, John	28	1833	Killcranny	St John	P
DEVANNY, William	21	1833	Killcranny	St John	RC
McCLANE, Daniel	22	1834	Castletoodry	Philadelphia	P
McCLANE, Hugh	20	1834	Castletoodry	Philadelphia	P
McLAUGHLIN, Thomas	22	1834	Drumaquill	Philadelphia	RC

COUNTY: LONDONDERRY
PARISH: KILREA

NAME	AGE	YEAR LEFT	TOWNLAND	DESTINATION	RELI- GION
COCHRAN, Robert	60	1834	Kilrea	Quebec	S
COCHRAN, Margaret	50	1834	Kilrea	Quebec	S
COCHRAN, Margaret Jun.	20	1834	Kilrea	Quebec	S
COCHRAN, Henry	23	1834	Kilrea	Quebec	S
COCHRAN, Jane	25	1834	Kilrea	Quebec	S
COCHRAN, Mary	27	1834	Kilrea	Quebec	S
MITCHELL, William	30	1834	Kilrea	Quebec	P
CRAIG, John	60	1834	Kilrea	Quebec	P
CRAIG, Sarah	55	1834	Kilrea	Quebec	P
CRAIG, Agnes	22	1834	Kilrea	Quebec	P
CRAIG, James	24	1834	Kilrea	Quebec	P
CRAIG, Mary Anne	19	1834	Kilrea	Quebéc	P
CRAIG, Alexander	16	1834	Kilrea	Quebec	P
CRAIG, William	12	1834	Kilrea	Quebec	P
McKEE, John	30	1834	Kilrea	Quebec	P
McKEE, Mary	30	1834	Kilrea	Quebec	P
McKEE, John Jun.	12	1834	Kilrea	Quebec	P
McKEE, Alexander	10	1834	Kilrea	Quebec	P
McKEE, Thomas	8	1834	Kilrea	Quebec	P
McKEE, Rachael	4	1834	Kilrea	Quebec	P
McHENRY, Betty	65	1834	Kilrea	Quebec	P
MOONEY, Betty	50	1834	Kilrea	Quebec	P
McKEEVER, Archy	16	1834	Kilrea	Quebec	RC
McKEEVER, Mary	19	1834	Kilrea	Quebec	RC
McKEEVER, Jane	14	1834	Kilrea	Quebec	RC
McKEEVER, Patrick	12	1834	Kilrea	Quebec	RC
McKEEVER, Martha Anne	7	1834	Kilrea	Quebec	RC
PATTERSON, Robert	30	1834	Kilrea	Quebec	RC
PATTERSON, Nancy	27	1834	Kilrea	Quebec	RC
PATTERSON, Samuel	15	1834	Kilrea	Quebec	RC
PATTERSON, Margret	4	1834	Kilrea	Quebec	RC
GRAHAM, James	45	1834	Kilrea	Quebec	RC
GRAHAM, Samuel	22	1834	Kilrea	Quebec	P
GRAHAM, William	24	1834	Kilrea	Quebec	P
GRAHAM, Anne	26	1834	Kilrea	Quebec	P
GRAHAM, John	18	1834	Kilrea	Quebec	P
GRAHAM, Sally	15	1834	Kilrea	Quebec	P
GRAHAM, Nancy	13	1834	Kilrea	Quebec	P
GRAHAM, James	9	1834	Kilrea	Quebec	P
GRAHAM, Robert	7	1834	Kilrea	Quebec	P
DIAMOND, Patrick	60	1834	Kilrea	Quebec	RC
DIAMOND, John	30	1834	Kilrea	Quebec	RC
DIAMOND, James	28	1834	Kilrea	Quebec	RC
DIAMOND, Margaret	26	1834	Kilrea	Quebec	RC
DIAMOND, Rose	24	1834	Kilrea	Quebec	RC
DIAMOND, Jane	22	1834	Kilrea	Quebec	RC
DIAMOND, Ellen	20	1834	Kilrea	Quebec	RC
DIAMOND, Hugh	18	1834	Kilrea	Quebec	RC
DIAMOND, William	14	1834	Kilrea	Quebec	RC
DIAMOND, Rose	16	1834	Kilrea	Quebec	RC
DIAMOND, Anne	11	1834	Kilrea	Quebec	RC
SMITH, Nancy	28	1834	Kilrea	Quebec	EC
ROBINSON, George	24	1834	Kilrea	Quebec	RC
PATTON, Mathew	35	1834	Kilrea	Quebec	P
PATTON, Nancy	35	1834	Kilrea	Quebec	P
PATTON, Henry	30	1834	Kilrea	Quebec	P
PATTON, William	20	1834	Kilrea	Quebec	P
PATTON, Nancy Jun.	12	1834	Kilrea	Quebec	P
PATTON, Sarah	10	1834	Kilrea	Quebec	P
PATTON, Martha	87	1834	Kilrea	Quebec	P
MOORE, Elizabeth	50	1834	Kilrea	Quebec	P
STEPHENSON, Diana	18	1834	Kilrea	Quebec	EC
McCANN, Martha	22	1834	Kilrea	Quebec	P
McCANN, Elizabeth	20	1834	Kilrea	Quebec	P

ORDNANCE SURVEY MEMOIRS

COUNTY: LONDONDERRY
PARISH: KILREA

NAME	AGE	YEAR LEFT	TOWNLAND	DESTINATION	RELI-GION
McCANN, Thomas	18	1834	Kilrea	Quebec	P
REID, Joseph	22	1834	Mynock	Quebec	P
REID, Mary	22	1834	Mynock	Quebec	P
ELLIOT, William	23	1834	Mynock	Quebec	P
ANDERSON, Margaret	24	1834	Mynock	Quebec	P
HENRY, Francis	35	1834	Mynock	New York	P
HENRY, Thomas	22	1834	Mynock	New York	P
CASSIDY, Frank	30	1834	Mullan	New York	RC
DIAMOND, James	20	1834	Movanagher	New York	RC
HEGGARTY, John	27	1834	Movanagher	New York	RC
DARAGH, Sarah	30	1834	Kilrea	Scotland (Returned)	RC
DAVIDSON, Catherine	45	1835	Kilrea	Quebec	EC
BROWN, Robert	15	1835	Kilrea	Quebec	EC
BELL, Jane	25	1835	Kilrea	Quebec	EC
BROWN, John	12	1835	Kilrea	Quebec	EC
MULHOLLAND, Elizabeth	18	1835	Kilrea	Quebec	EC
CORRISTON, Jane	60	1835	Kilrea	Quebec	RC
CORRISTON, Catherine	20	1835	Kilrea	Quebec	RC
CORRISTON, William	25	1835	Kilrea	Quebec	RC
IRWIN, William	22	1835	Mynock	Quebec	P
HENRY, Elizabeth	60	1835	Mynock	New York	EC
BRADLEY, Mary	25	1835	Mynock	New York	RC
BRADLEY, Patrick	26	1835	Mynock	New York	RC
McCAHEY, Nathaniel	21	1835	Mynock	St John	P
DUNLOP, Ellen Jane	22	1835	Mynock	St John	P
DUNLOP, Matilda	19	1835	Mynock	St John	P
DUNBAR, Mary	40	1835	Mynock	St John	P
DUNBAR, Mary Sen.	60	1835	Mynock	St John	P
DUNBAR, Mary Jun.	30	1835	Mynock	St John	P
DUNBAR, Margaret	6	1835	Mynock	St John	P
DUNBAR, Jane	4	1835	Mynock	St John	P
CAMPBELL, John	22	1835	Fallahogy	Philadelphia	P
COLE, James	30	1835	Kilrea	Philadelphia	RC
COLE, Ellen	25	1835	Kilrea	Philadelphia	RC
COLE, James	2	1835	Kilrea	Philadelphia	RC
HAGAN, Margaret	28	1835	Kilrea	Philadelphia	RC

ORDNANCE SURVEY MEMOIRS

COUNTY: LONDONDERRY
PARISH: LISSAN

NAME	AGE	YEAR LEFT	TOWNLAND	DESTINATION	RELI-GION
GLASCO, James	29	1834	Coltrim	New York	P
LADDEN, John	40	1834	Coltrim	Quebec	RC
LADDEN, Sarah	20	1834	Coltrim	Quebec	RC
LADDEN, Bernard	6mths	1834	Coltrim	Quebec	RC
McANANA, Robert	22	1834	Coltrim	Quebec	RC
DEVLIN, John	19	1834	Coltrim	Philadelphia	RC
McKENNA, Margaret	29	1834	Dunnabraggy	Quebec	RC
McCREE, Mary	27	1834	Dunnabraggy	Philadelphia	P
McCULLAGH, Samuel	34	1834	Drumeen	Philadelphia	P
HARKNESS, John	31	1834	Drumard	Philadelphia	P
McCULLAGH, Archibald	30	1834	Lissan Demesne	Philadelphia	P
O'NEIL, Francis	40	1834	Tullynure	Philadelphia	P
McANANA, James	26	1834	Tullynure	New York	RC
HUTCHISON, Sarah	42	1834	Tullynure	New York	RC
HUTCHISON, Hugh	20	1834	Tullynure	New York	RC
HUTCHISON, Mary	25	1834	Tullynure	New York	RC
HUTCHISON, Nancy	26	1834	Ballyforles	New York	RC
BONNETT, John	56	1834	Claggan	Quebec	RC
BONNETT, Adam	32	1834	Claggan	Quebec	RC
BONNETT, Samuel	30	1834	Claggan	Quebec	RC
BONNETT, James	10	1834	Claggan	Quebec	RC
BONNETT, Martha	25	1834	Claggan	Quebec	RC
McCLEESE, Thomas	18	1834	Claggan	Quebec	RC
MILLS, Mathew	32	1834	Caneese	New York (Returned)	P
McCANN, Susan	23	1834	Tintagh	New York	RC
HEANY, Patrick	24	1834	Tintagh	Baltimore	RC
HAGAN, Peter	27	1834	Tintagh	Dundee	RC
McGURNEY, James	26	1834	Letteran	Quebec	S
CAMPBELL, Peter	30	1834	Diran	New York	RC
GLASCO, William	29	1835	Coltrim	New York	P
DEVLIN, Mary	24	1835	Coltrim	Quebec	RC
IRWIN, Stewart	29	1835	Killybasky	Quebec	P
McCULLAGH, Jane	26	1835	Drumard	Philadelphia	P
CARSON, Alexander	40	1835	Knockadoo	New York	P
CARSON, Esther	35	1835	Knockadoo	New York	P
HUNTER, Elizabeth	25	1835	Knockadoo	New York	P

COUNTY: LONDONDERRY

PARISH: LISSAN

SEASONAL MIGRANTS

NAME	AGE	YEAR LEFT	TOWNLAND	DESTINATION	RELI-GION
McCANN, William	25		Coltrim	Glasgow	P
DEVLIN, Patrick	33		Coltrim	Glasgow	RC
DUNSHEATH, James	30		Coltrim	Glasgow	P
CRAWFORD, Robert	25		Coltrim	Glasgow	P
McANNA, Patrick	25		Coltrim	Glasgow	RC
WARD, Daniel	30		Coltrim	Glasgow	RC
COWAN, Thomas	48		Coltrim	Glasgow	RC
DEVLIN, Jane	45		Coltrim	Glasgow	RC
DONELLY, Bernard	45		Muff	Glasgow	RC
GREENAN, John	60		Moneyhaw	Glasgow	RC
GREENAN, Jeremiah	35		Moneyhaw	Glasgow	RC
GREENAN, William	20		Moneyhaw	Glasgow	RC
McMASTER, John	30		Moneyhaw	Glasgow	P
DONNELLY, Hugh	35		Moneyhaw	Glasgow	RC
QUINN, Charles	48		Moneyhaw	Glasgow	RC
BELL, Robert	45		Killybaskey	Merryport	P
TONER, John	50		Drummeen	Glasgow	RC
WRIGHT, Joseph	16		Claggan	Glasgow	P
MITCHELL, John	20		Claggan	Glasgow	P
SHERRY, Edward	22		Knockadoo	Glasgow	RC
SHERRY, Bernard	32		Knockadoo	Glasgow	RC
McKERNAN, John	20		Knockadoo	Glasgow	RC
McCULLAGH, Christopher	40		Knockadoo	Glasgow	RC
McCULLAGH, Mary	40		Knockadoo	Glasgow	RC
HAGAN, Eliza	21		Knockadoo	Glasgow	RC
McCULLAGH, Nancy	18		Knockadoo	Glasgow	RC
HAGAN, Peter	25		Tintagh	Glasgow	RC
HAGAN, Nancy	25		Tintagh	Glasgow	RC
DOYLE, John	35		Tintagh	Glasgow	RC
DOYLE, Philip	20		Tintagh	Glasgow	RC
DOYLE, Mary	32		Tintagh	Glasgow	RC
DOYLE, Margaret	17		Tintagh	Glasgow	RC
DOYLE, John	15		Tintagh	Glasgow	RC
HOGAN, John	36		Letteran	Glasgow	RC
HOGAN, Mary	26		Letteran	Glasgow	RC
HOGAN, Martha	32		Letteran	Glasgow	RC
DEVLIN, Jane	26		Letteran	Glasgow	RC
MULLAN, Patrick	40		Dernan	Glasgow	RC
MULLAN, Nancy	40		Dernan	Glasgow	RC
MULLAN, Patrick	20		Dernan	Glasgow	RC
FRIEL, John	44		Dernan	Glasgow	RC
FRIEL, John Jun.	24		Dernan	Glasgow	RC
FARRELL, James	45		Dernan	Glasgow	RC
DUGAN, John	30		Dernan	Glasgow	RC
MULLAN, Michael	28		Dernan	Glasgow	RC
CAMPBELL, Patrick	30		Dernan	Glasgow	RC
MULLAN, John	34		Dernan	Glasgow	RC
MULLAN, Martha	40		Dernan	Glasgow	RC
MULLAN, Peter	26		Dernan	Glasgow	RC
MULLAN, Michael	25		Dernan	Glasgow	RC
MULLAN, Michael	32		Derryganard	Glasgow	RC
McCONVEY, John	30		Derryganard	Glasgow	RC
McCONVEY, Charles	32		Derryganard	Glasgow	RC
MULLAN, Bernard	25		Derryganard	Glasgow	RC
MULLAN, Charles	30		Derryganard	Glasgow	RC
MULLAN, Margaret	50		Derryganard	Glasgow	RC
O'NEIL, Felix	28		Derryganard	Glasgow	RC
O'NEIL, Bridget	28		Derryganard	Glasgow	RC
O'NEIL, James	26		Derryganard	Glasgow	RC
O'NEIL, Bridget	30		Derryganard	Glasgow	RC
McGLADE, Robert	40		Rossmore	Liverpool	RC

COUNTY: LONDONDERRY
PARISH: MACOSQUIN

NAME	AGE	YEAR LEFT	TOWNLAND	DESTINATION	RELI- GION
McMASTER, Alexander	28	1834	Camus	Philadelphia	P
McENTIRE, Robert	27	1834	Camus	Philadelphia	P
McENTIRE, Thomas	26	1834	Camus	Charlestown	P
PATTON, Samuel	26	1833	Gills	Quebec	P
PATTON, Anne	24	1833	Gills	Quebec	P
PATTON, Mary	5	1833	Gills	Quebec	P
STEWART, Margaret Anne	18	1834	Curragh	Philadelphia	P
MARTIN, Samuel	30	1833	Carndougan	Philadelphia	P
McMULLEN, Alexander	28	1833	Carndougan	Philadelphia	P
McMULLEN, William	24	1834	Carndougan	Philadelphia	P
FINLAY, Robert	24	1833	Castleroe	Quebec	P
FINLAY, Mary	23	1833	Castleroe	Quebec	P
CUNNINGHAM, William	17	1833	Castleroe	Quebec	P
PATTON, William	26	1834	Ballylintagh	New York	RC
McQUIGGY, Arthur	40	1834	Farranlester	New York	RC
McQUIGGY, Margaret	20	1834	Farranlester	New York	RC
FARGEY, John	20	1834	Farranlester	St John	P
HARPER, James	21	1834	Glenleary	Quebec	P
BLAIR, Robert	20	1834	Ballinteer South	Quebec	P
BLAIR, John	18	1834	Ballinteer South	Quebec	P
HUSTON, Elizabeth	36	1834	Ballinteer South	Philadelphia	P
GORDON, James	28	1834	Killure	St John	P
USHER, John	24	1834	Killure	St John	P
MORRISON, Mathew	27	1834	Crossgare	St John	P
POLLOCK, George	21	1834	Ringrashmore	Quebec	P
KENEDY, Mathew	24	1834	Ringrashmore	Quebec	P
KING, William	24	1834	Ballyvennox	Quebec	P
TRAINOR, Thomas	26	1833	Ballintagh	Quebec	P
MILLER, Jane	20	1833	Arvarness	St John	P
ANDERSON, David	22	1833	Arvarness	St John	P
ANDERSON, Margretanne	1	1833	Arvarness	St John	P
McCAULLA, Catherine	18	1834	Arvarness	Philadelphia	P
McCAULLA, Isabella	16	1834	Arvarness	Philadelphia	P
MILLER, John	21	1834	Kiltinny Lower	Philadelphia	P
BOOTH, Thomas	19	1833	Cam	St John	P
McGONIGLE, Thomas	18	1834	Cam	Philadelphia	P
HUNTER, David	32	1834	Leck	Philadelphia	P
HUNTER, Hanah	24	1834	Leck	Philadelphia	P
POLLOCK, James	44	1834	Leck	Quebec	P
POLLOCK, Ann	42	1834	Leck	Quebec	P
POLLOCK, Jane	18	1834	Leck	Quebec	P
POLLOCK, Martha	16	1834	Leck	Quebec	P
POLLOCK, Ann	12	1834	Leck	Quebec	P
POLLOCK, James	9	1834	Leck	Quebec	P
POLLOCK, Eliza	7	1834	Leck	Quebec	P
POLLOCK, Robert	5	1834	Leck	Quebec	P
POLLOCK, James	24	1834	Leck	Quebec	P
POLLOCK, John	22	1834	Leck	Quebec	P
POLLOCK, George	34	1834	Leck	Quebec	P
POLLOCK, Maryane	28	1834	Leck	Quebec	P
BLACK, James	40	1834	Cashel	Quebec	P
BLACK, Eliza	42	1834	Cashel	Quebec	P
BLACK, William	14	1834	Cashel	Quebec	P
BLACK, Hugh	12	1834	Cashel	Quebec	P
BLACK, Robert	10	1834	Cashel	Quebec	P
BLACK, Ann	18	1834	Cashel	Quebec	P
BLACK, Eliza	16	1834	Cashel	Quebec	P

ORDNANCE SURVEY MEMOIRS

COUNTY: LONDONDERRY
PARISH: MAGHERA

NAME	AGE	YEAR LEFT	TOWNLAND	DESTINATION	RELI-GION
MARTIN, John	38	1834	Ballymacross	New York	P
McCAHEY, James	28	1834	Ballymacross	New York	P
FLEMMING, James	17	1834	Ballymacross	St John	P
FLEMMING, Sarah	15	1834	Ballymacross	St John	P
FLEMMING, Andrew	24	1834	Ballymacross	St John	P
BARR, William	20	1834	Ballynahone Beg	Quebec	P
MARTIN, William	20	1834	Ballynahone Beg	Quebec	P
BARR, Catherine	19	1834	Ballynahone Beg	Quebec	P
MARTIN, Jane	24	1834	Ballynahone Beg	Quebec	P
LORIMER, James	56	1834	Ballynahone Beg	Quebec (returned 1835)	P
BRADLEY, Robert	36	1834	Ballynahone Beg	Liverpool	RC
McALANE, Sarah	22	1834	Curran	New York	RC
McALANE, Jane	26	1834	Curran	New York	RC
STURGEON, John	18	1834	Toberhead	Quebec	P
LEE, John	25	1834	Toberhead	Quebec	P
LEE, Mary	20	1834	Toberhead	Quebec	P
STONE, Robert	20	1834	Toberhead	Quebec	P
STONE, Jane	24	1834	Toberhead	Quebec	P
CAMPBELL, William	20	1834	Toberhead	Quebec	P
CONROY, Mary	25	1834	Rocktown	Philadelphia	RC
MILLER, Sarah	20	1834	Rocktown	Philadelphia	RC
McKENNA, Bridget	8	1834	Fallagloon	New York	RC
McKENNA, Margret	6	1834	Fallagloon	New York	RC
McKENNA, Peter	11	1834	Fallagloon	New York	RC
McKENNA, John	9	1834	Fallagloon	New York	RC
CASSIDY, Frank	24	1834	Fallagloon	New York	RC
McCLOSKEY, Sarah	26	1834	Fallagloon	New York	RC
McWILLIAMS, Felix	25	1834	Fallagloon	Quebec	RC
McBRIDE, Andrew	22	1834	Fallagloon	New York	RC
BRADLEY, John	20	1834	Fallagloon	Philadelphia	RC
WILSON, Joseph	20	1834	Tirgarvel	Quebec	P
WILSON, Hannah	19	1834	Tirgarvel	Quebec	P
WILSON, Mary	6mths	1834	Tirgarvel	Quebec	P
BRADLEY, James	40	1834	Tirgarvel	Quebec	RC
HESSAN, William	20	1834	Tirgarvel	Quebec	RC
HESSAN, Nanny	22	1834	Tirgarvel	Quebec	RC
HESSAN, Edward	16	1834	Tirgarvel	Quebec	RC
HESSAN, John	13	1834	Tirgarvel	Quebec	RC
HESSAN, Frank	9	1834	Tirgarvel	Quebec	RC
HESSAN, Mary	15	1834	Tirgarvel	Quebec	RC
HESSAN, Margret	7	1834	Tirgarvel	Quebec	RC
SWEENY, Patrick	22	1834	Tirgarvel	Quebec	RC
TOGHILL, James	20	1834	Drummuck	Philadelphia	RC
TOGHILL, Michael	18	1834	Drummuck	Philadelphia	RC
TOGHILL, Peter	16	1834	Drummuck	Philadelphia	RC
TOGHILL, Nancy	14	1834	Drummuck	Philadelphia	RC
MAGUIGAN, Patrick	30	1834	Drummuck	Philadelphia	RC
McNEIL, Andrew	18	1834	Dunglady	Quebec	RC
KENNY, William	20	1834	Dunglady	Quebec	RC
MOONEY, John	26	1834	Falgortrevy	Quebec	RC
McCONAGHTY, John	26	1834	Craigadick	Quebec	RC
McFLINN, Neil	40	1834	Falgortrevy	Quebec	RC
McFLINN, Hugh	35	1834	Falgortrevy	Quebec	RC
DONAGHOE, James	26	1834	Macknagh	Quebec	RC
MULHOLLAND, David	40	1834	Macknagh	Quebec	RC
McSHANE, Rose	25	1834	Macknagh	Quebec	RC
ORR, James	25	1834	Curragh	Quebec	P
DYART, Robert	19	1834	Curragh	Quebec	P
ANDERSON, William	30	1834	Curragh	Quebec	P
MAGOWAN, Mary	25	1834	Curragh	Quebec	P
ORR, Elizabeth	50	1834	Curragh	Quebec	P
DOHERTY, Mary	26	1834	Fallagloon	Philadelphia	RC
McWILLIAMS, Daniel	24	1834	Fallagloon	St John	RC

89

COUNTY: LONDONDERRY
PARISH: MAGHERA

NAME	AGE	YEAR LEFT	TOWNLAND	DESTINATION	RELI-GION
McWILLIAMS, Donald	27	1834	Fallagloon	Quebec	RC
McKENNA, James	50	1834	Fallagloon	New York	RC
McKENNA, John	14	1834	Fallagloon	New York	RC
McKENNA, Nanny	10	1834	Fallagloon	New York	RC
MOORE, Thomas	18	1834	Fallagloon	Quebec	P
HUSTON, Robert	19	1834	Fallagloon	Quebec	P
POOL, John	35	1834	Town of Maghera	Quebec	P
POOL, Hannah	36	1834	Town of Maghera	Quebec	P
POOL, James	10	1834	Town of Maghera	Quebec	P
POOL, John	8	1834	Town of Maghera	Quebec	P
POOL, Samuel	6	1834	Town of Maghera	Quebec	P
POOL, Mathew	5	1834	Town of Maghera	Quebec	P
POOL, Robert	4	1834	Town of Maghera	Quebec	P
POOL, Anne	3	1834	Town of Maghera	Quebec	P
POOL, Jane	1	1834	Town of Maghera	Quebec	P
MOONEY, John	22	1834	Town of Maghera	Quebec	P
MOONEY, Jane	21	1834	Town of Maghera	Quebeo	P
HUSTON, John	25	1834	Ballymacilcurr	Quebec	RC
HUSTON, Henry	50	1834	Ballymacilcurr	Quebec	RC
WINTON, William	25	1834	Ballymacilcurr	Philadelphia	RC
WINTON, Ellen	24	1834	Ballymacilcurr	Philadelphia	RC
WINTON, Jane	22	1834	Ballymacilcurr	Philadelphia	RC
WILSON, Thomas	22	1834	Ballymacilcurr	Philadelphia	RC
HUSTON, John	35	1834	Ballymacilcurr	Philadelphia	RC
HUSTON, Betty	26	1834	Ballymacilcurr	Philadelphia	RC
HUSTON, Sally	12	1834	Ballymacilcurr	Philadelphia	RC
HUSTON, Anne Jane	10	1834	Ballymacilcurr	Philadelphia	RC
HUSTON, John Jun	2	1834	Ballymacilcurr	Philadelphia	RC
HUSTON, Charles	5	1834	Ballymacilcurr	Philadelphia	RC
ORR, Daniel	12	1834	Curragh	Quebec	P
ORR, Mary	10	1834	Curragh	Quebec	P
ORR, Alexander	9	1834	Curragh	Quebec	P
ORR, William	7	1834	Curragh	Quebec	P
ANDERSON, George	50	1834	Slaghtybogy	Philadelphia	P
ANDERSON, Jane	40	1834	Slaghtybogy	Philadelphia	P
ANDERSON, William	14	1834	Slaghtybogy	Philadelphia	P
ANDERSON, David	12	1834	Slaghtybogy	Philadelphia	P
ANDERSON, Martha	10	1834	Slaghtybogy	Philadelphia	P
ANDERSON, Barbara	13	1834	Slaghtybogy	Philadelphia	P
ANDERSON, Isabella	8	1834	Slaghtybogy	Philadelphia	P
ANDERSON, Sarah	6	1834	Slaghtybogy	Philadelphia	P
ANDERSON, Mathew	16	1834	Slaghtybogy	Philadelphia	P
ANDERSON, Nathaniel	21	1834	Slaghtybogy	Philadelphia	P
MAGUIGGAN, Patrick	22	1834	Drumconready	New York	RC
MITCHELL, John	35	1835	Beagh (Spiritual)	Quebec	S
PETTIGREW, Thomas	30	1835	Beagh (Spiritual)	Quebec	S
PETTIGREW, Robert	18	1835	Beagh (Spiritual)	Quebec	S
McCLOSKEY, Sarah	23	1835	Moneymore	New York	RC
McCOOL, John	20	1835	Toberhead	Van Dieman's Land	P
REYNOLDS, Anne	30	1835	Toberhead	Quebec	EC
HENDERSON, Robert	19	1835	Town of Maghera	New York	P
LAGAN, Sarah	25	1835	Town of Maghera	New Orleans	RC
LAGAN, Hugh	20	1835	Town of Maghera	New Orleans	RC
McCLOSKEY, Margaret	20	1835	Town of Maghera	Quebec	RC
WINTON, Jane	23	1835	Town of Maghera	Quebec	EC
MAGOWAN, Patrick	24	1835	Gorteade	Quebec	RC
MAGOWAN, Henry	24	1835	Gorteade	Quebec	RC
LAFFERTY, Margaret	12	1835	Gorteade	Quebec	RC
LAFFERTY, Mary	16	1835	Gorteade	Quebec	RC
O'KANE, Patrick	22	1835	Gorteade	Quebec	RC
McMASTER, James	18	1835	Gorteade	Quebec	RC
McMASTER, Ann	20	1835	Gorteade	Quebec	RC
SMITH, Andrew	30	1835	Upperland	Quebec	P
SMITH, Ellen	25	1835	Upperland	Quebec	P

ORDNANCE SURVEY MEMOIRS

NAME	AGE	YEAR LEFT	TOWNLAND	DESTINATION	RELI- GION
SMITH, John	1¾	1835	Upperland	Quebec	P
JARVIS, Catherine	20	1835	Upperland	Quebec	P
LOGAN, James	60	1835	Upperland	Quebec	P
LOGAN, Margaret	60	1835	Upperland	Quebec	P
LOGAN, Mary	30	1835	Upperland	Quebec	P
LOGAN, Hannah	28	1835	Upperland	Quebec	P
LOGAN, William	26	1835	Upperland	Quebec	P
LOGAN, John	24	1835	Upperland	Quebec	P
LOGAN, Nancy	22	1835	Upperland	Quebec	P
WINTON, Ellen	24	1835	Ballymacilcurr	Philadelphia	P
WINTON, Jane	22	1835	Ballymacilcurr	Philadelphia	P
PAUL, Martha	14	1835	Crew	Philadelphia	P
PAUL, Jane	18	1835	Crew	Philadelphia	P
DEVLIN, Paul	22	1835	Drumconready	Van Dieman's Land	RC
McKENNA, John	21	1835	Drumconready	Van Dieman's Land	RC
KEITH, James	42	1835	Lisnamuck	Philadelphia	RC
QUINN, John	30	1835	Beagh Temporal	New York	RC
QUINN, Frank	18	1835	Beagh Temporal	New York	RC
HAMILTON, Alexander	32	1835	Swatragh	New York	EC

COUNTY: LONDONDERRY

PARISH: MAGHERA

NAME	AGE	YEAR LEFT	TOWNLAND	DESTINATION	RELI-GION
HANNAN, John	35		Culnagrew	Glasgow	RC
HANNAN, John	31		Culnagrew	Glasgow	RC
HANNAN, Henry Jun	28		Culnagrew	Glasgow	RC
KANE, Edward	30		Culnagrew	Glasgow	RC
McSHANE, Felix	21		Culnagrew	Glasgow	RC
McLAUGHLIN, John	28		Culnagrew	Glasgow	RC
McLAUGHLIN, Patrick	45		Culnagrew	Glasgow	RC
McATAMNEY, John	36		Culnagrew	Glasgow	RC
McATAMNEY, Neil	22		Culnagrew	Glasgow	RC
McATAMNEY, Patrick	20		Culnagrew	Glasgow	RC
McLAUGHLIN, Bernard	50		Culnagrew	Glasgow	RC
McSHANE, Peter	33		Culnagrew	Glasgow	RC
CRILLY, James	23		Culnagrew	Glasgow	RC
QUINN, Michael	20		Culnagrew	Glasgow	RC
McKEEFRY, Patrick	24		Culnagrew	Glasgow	RC
McKEEFRY, Michael	28		Culnagrew	Glasgow	RC
MELLON, Edward	40		Keady	Glasgow	RC
McQUILLAN, Michael	25		Keady	Glasgow	RC
LOUGHLIN, Joseph	50		Keady	Glasgow	RC
O'KANE, Frank	40		Keady	Glasgow	RC
O'KANE, Peter	35		Keady	Glasgow	RC
O'KANE, Peter Jun	30		Keady	Glasgow	RC
MAGOWAN, Thomas	28		Keady	Glasgow	RC
MAGOWAN, Michael	25		Keady	Glasgow	RC
DOHERTY, Frank	24		Keady	Glasgow	RC
CASSIDY, John	30		Fallagloon	Glasgow	RC
MAGUCKIAN, Thomas	22		Fallagloon	Glasgow	RC
MAGUCKIAN, John Sen	60		Fallagloon	Glasgow	RC
MAGUCKIAN, John Jun	18		Fallagloon	Glasgow	RC
SHARKEY, James	25		Fallagloon	Glasgow	RC
DOHERTY, Hugh	32		Drummuck	Glasgow	RC
MAGOWAN, John	40		Drummuck	Glasgow	RC
MULHOLLAND, William	25		Drummuck	Glasgow	RC
MULHOLLAND, John	40		Drummuck	Glasgow	RC
HEGARTY, Bernard	30		Drummuck	Glasgow	RC
MILLICAN, John	40		Drummuck	Glasgow	RC
McSHANE, John	26		Drummuck	Glasgow	RC
BRADLEY, William	40		Drummuck	Glasgow	RC
DEVLIN, Michael	35		Drummuck	Glasgow	RC
MADIGAN, John	23		Drummuck	Glasgow	RC
McMULLAN, Edward	22		Drummuck	Glasgow	RC
McMULLAN, Patrick	2C		Drummuck	Glasgow	RC
DOHERTY, Frank	40		Drummuck	Glasgow	RC
CLARK, Nat	45		Drummuck	Glasgow	RC
CLARK, James	18		Drummuck	Glasgow	RC
DOWNEY, Edward	25		Drummuck	Glasgow	RC
DOWNEY, John	22		Drummuck	Glasgow	RC
TOGHILL, Daniel	20		Drummuck	Glasgow	RC
CONNELLY, Mathew	40		Drummuck	Glasgow	RC
CRILLY, Hugh	22		Gorteade	Glasgow	RC
CRILLY, James	24		Gorteade	Glasgow	RC
MILLAR, Patrick	30		Gorteade	Glasgow	RC
MAGOWAN, Michael	26		Gorteade	Glasgow	RC
LAFFERTY, Hugh	21		Gorteade	Glasgow	RC
LYNN, Hugh	20		Gorteade	Glasgow	RC
QUIGLEY, John	26		Drumard	Glasgow	RC
CONWAY, Peter	28		Drumard	Glasgow	RC
QUIGLEY, Patrick	28		Drumard	Glasgow	RC
HUGHES, Edward	26		Drumard	Glasgow	RC
McKEIGNEY, Patrick	22		Drumard	Glasgow	RC
DOHERTY, Patrick	23		Drumard	Glasgow	RC
KELLY, Peter	45		Gulladuff	Glasgow	RC
HELFERTY, Samuel	44		Gulladuff	Glasgow	RC
CASSIDY, Charles	22		Dreenan	Glasgow	RC

COUNTY: LONDONDERRY

SEASONAL MIGRANTS

PARISH: MAGHERA

NAME	AGE	YEAR LEFT	TOWNLAND	DESTINATION	RELI-GION
CONNOR, John	40		Dreenan	Glasgow	RC
NEIL, Edward	24		Dreenan	Glasgow	RC
McGOLDRAKE, Patrick	22		Dreenan	Glasgow	RC
HENRY, Bernard	26		Dreenan	Glasgow	RC
HENRY, Henry	28		Dreenan	Glasgow	RC
O'HARA, James	40		Dreenan	Glasgow	RC
McALISTER, James	25		Dreenan	Glasgow	RC
DOHERTY, Henry	24		Dreenan	Glasgow	RC
FARRELL, Henry	30		Dreenan	Glasgow	RC
DOWNEY, Edward	24		Dreenan	Glasgow	RC
BULL, Edward	22		Dreenan	Glasgow	RC
HAMMEL, John	25		Dreenan	Glasgow	RC
HAMMEL, Patrick	23		Dreenan	Glasgow	RC
NEIL, Bernard	26		Dreenan	Glasgow	RC
NEIL, Arthur	24		Dreenan	Glasgow	RC
NEIL, Henry	28		Dreenan	Glasgow	RC
HENRY, Patrick	27		Dreenan	Glasgow	RC
HENRY, Frank	24		Dreenan	Glasgow	RC
HEGARTY, William	25		Dreenan	Glasgow	RC
HENRY, Thomas	40		Dreenan	Glasgow	RC
HENRY, Dominick	26		Dreenan	Glasgow	RC
BRITAIN, Neil	24		Dreenan	Glasgow	RC
MULLAN, Patrick	25		Dreenan	Glasgow	RC
DONAHOE, Edward	22		Macknagh	Glasgow	RC
McSHANE, Andrew	25		Macknagh	Glasgow	RC
McQUILLAN, Thomas	25		Macknagh	Glasgow	RC
McTAMNEY, David	25		Macknagh	Glasgow	RC
McQUILLAN, Arwley	25		Macknagh	Glasgow	RC
SHARKEY, Michael	30		Fallagloon	Glasgow	RC
SHARKEY, Thomas	56		Fallagloon	Glasgow	RC
CONVERY, John	32		Fallagloon	Glasgow	RC
CONVERY, Michael	30		Fallagloon	Glasgow	RC
CONVERY, James	25		Fallagloon	Glasgow	RC
MORAN, Michael	18		Fallagloon	Glasgow	RC
KEARNEY, John	26		Fallagloon	Glasgow	RC
JOHNSTONE, Henry	20		Fallagloon	Glasgow	EC
McALISTER, John	24		Fallagloon	Glasgow	RC
LAGAN, John	30		Lisnamuck	Liverpool	RC
LAGAN, Thomas	20		Lisnamuck	Liverpool	RC
McGLADE, John	25		Drumconready	Glasgow	RC
McCORMICK, Rodger	38		Drumconready	Glasgow	RC
McCORMICK, Jenkin	44		Bracknagrilly	Glasgow	RC
CONVERY, James	56		Kirley	Liverpool	RC
CONVERY, Hugh	25		Kirley	Liverpool	RC
CONVERY, Edward	24		Kirley	Liverpool	RC
McATAMNEY, Denis	20		Moyagall	Glasgow	RC
McATAMNEY, Edward	30		Moyagall	Glasgow	RC
McKENNA, James	40		Moyagall	Glasgow	RC
CONVERY, Henry	30		Moyagall	Glasgow	RC
McANALLY, James	24		Moyagall	Glasgow	RC
MAGEE, James	22		Moyagall	Glasgow	RC
CONVERY, John	24		Moyagall	Glasgow	RC
CONVERY, Patrick	20		Moyagall	Glasgow	RC
CONVERY, John	40		Moyagall	Glasgow	RC
McCANN, Edward	25		Moyagall	Glasgow	RC
CALDWELL, Neil	25		Moyagall	Glasgow	RC
McCLARNAN, Thomas	22		Moyagall	Glasgow	RC
CONVERY, Bernard	24		Moyagall	Glasgow	RC
DURAS, John	40		Moyagall	Glasgow	RC
McILHATTON, Edward	26		Moyagall	Glasgow	RC
McILHATTON, Patrick	24		Moyagall	Glasgow	RC
CONVERY, Henry	24		Moyagall	Glasgow	RC
CONVERY, Frank	26		Moyagall	Glasgow	RC
McINTYRE, Arthur	26		Moyagall	Glasgow	RC

COUNTY: LONDONDERRY

PARISH: MAGHERA

NAME	AGE	YEAR LEFT	TOWNLAND	DESTINATION	RELI- GION
SCULLION, Peter	21		Moyagall	Glasgow	RC
BERRIMAN, John	24		Moyagall	Glasgow	RC
McKENNA, John	19		Moyagall	Glasgow	RC
McDEVITT, Patrick	19		Moyagall	Glasgow	RC
McKENNA, John	60		Moyagall	Glasgow	RC
CONVERY, Nicholas	26		Moyagall	Glasgow	RC
CONVERY, John	35		Moyagall	Glasgow	RC
McATAMNEY, John	25		Moyagall	Glasgow	RC
McKINLEY, Hugh	52		Crew	Liverpool	RC
McMULLAN, Edward	24		Drummuck	Glasgow	RC
MILLICAN, John	26		Drummuck	Glasgow	RC
MULHOLLAND, John	30		Drummuck	Glasgow	RC
BOYLE, John	25		Drummuck	Glasgow	RC
BOYLE, Nat	27		Drummuck	Glasgow	RC
MULHOLLAND, David	30		Drummuck	Glasgow	RC
BOYLE, Stephen	29		Drummuck	Glasgow	RC
CONVERY, William	26		Drummuck	Glasgow	RC
DONNELLY, Henry	24		Drummuck	Glasgow	RC
MONTIGUE, Michael	24		Drummuck	Glasgow	RC
MONTIGUE, Bernard	26		Drummuck	Glasgow	RC
MADDIGAN, John	19		Drummuck	Glasgow	RC
TOGHILL, Michael	26		Drummuck	Glasgow	RC
CONVERY, William	30		Drummuck	Glasgow	RC
BOYLE, Daniel	40		Drummuck	Glasgow	RC
O'NEIL, Frank	35		Drummuck	Glasgow	RC
DOHERTY, William	34		Drummuck	Glasgow	RC
MYNOGHER, Charles	20		Dunglady	Liverpool	RC
KEARNEY, James	30		Dunglady	Glasgow	RC
McPEAKE, Bernard	24		Swatragh	Glasgow	RC
BOND, John	26		Swatragh	Glasgow	EC
CRILLY, Arthur	27		Swatragh	Glasgow	RC
CRILLY, John	24		Swatragh	Glasgow	RC
BOND, Martha	30		Swatragh	Glasgow	EC
O'KANE, John	38		Swatragh	Liverpool	EC
KENNEDY, William	20		Culnady	Liverpool	P
WILLIAMSON, James	21		Culnady	Liverpool	P
ARBUTHNOT, John	20		Gorteade	Glasgow	P
McILWHINNEY, Patrick	24		Gorteade	Glasgow	P

COUNTY: LONDONDERRY
PARISH: MAGHERAFELT

NAME	AGE	YEAR LEFT	TOWNLAND	DESTINATION	RELI-GION
COSTELLO, Elizabeth	25	1834	Killyneese	Philadelphia	RC
SPICER, Samuel	14	1834	Ballynocker	Philadelphia	P
SILLIA, William	28	1834	Aghagaskin	Philadelphia	P
LOVE, Robert	20	1834	Tamnadeese	New Orleans	P
DUNCAN, Isabella	20	1834	Drumrainy	Quebec	P
KEESIE, Henry	18	1834	Glenmaguill	Quebec	EC
KENNY, John	60	1834	Magherafelt	Quebec	EC
KENNY, Sally Ann	26	1834	Magherafelt	Quebec	EC
KENNY, Mary	10	1834	Magherafelt	Quebec	EC
KENNY, Jane	58	1834	Magherafelt	Quebec	EC
KENNY, Jane	18	1834	Magherafelt	Quebec	EC
SIMPSON, Alexander	50	1834	Magherafelt	Quebec	EC
SIMPSON, George	19	1834	Magherafelt	Quebec	EC
SIMPSON, Mary	48	1834	Magherafelt	Quebec	EC
LAFFERTY, William	7	1834	Magherafelt	Quebec	EC
LEACOCK, James	20	1834	Magherafelt	Quebec	EC
CONN, James	19	1834	Magherafelt	New York	P
CAMPBELL, Bernard	18	1834	Magherafelt	New York	RC
DAYLY, Michael	28	1834	Magherafelt	New York	RC
BODEN, Sarah	20	1834	Leckagh	Pittsburgh	P
HUNTER, William	18	1834	Coolshinny	Quebec	P
CONN, John	16	1834	Magherafelt	Quebec	P
DEVLIN, Ann	20	1834	Magherafelt	Quebec	RC
BRADLEY, Elenor	20	1835	Killyneese	New York	RC
MORTON, David	18	1835	Ballynocker	Philadelphia	P
CHAMBERS, Elizabeth	30	1835	Aghagaskin	New York	P
SILLY, Thomas	21	1835	Glenmaquill	New Orleans	EC
KEESIE, Joseph	22	1835	Glenmaquill	Quebec	EC
KELLY, Ritchard	26	1835	Aghagaskin	New York	RC
McQUAID, Henry	27	1835	Magherafelt	New York	RC
McKEON, Murtagh	19	1835	Magherafelt	New York	RC
SMYTH, John	20	1835	Magherafelt	New York	EC
SIMMON, Maryann	20	1835	Magherafelt	Quebec	RC

COUNTY: LONDONDERRY
PARISH: MAGILLIGAN

NAME	AGE	YEAR LEFT	TOWNLAND	DESTINATION	RELI-GION
QUINN, John	19	1834	Ballymagoland	Quebec	RC
MELON, Jane	23	1834	Oughtymore	Philadelphia	RC
MELON, Nancy	25	1833	Oughtymore	Quebec	RC
DOHERTY, Jane	18	1834	Oughtymore	New York	RC
KELLY, William	20	1833	Ballyscullion	Philadelphia	EC
DOHERTY, William	22	1833	Ballyscullion	Philadelphia	RC
DOHERTY, Edward	25	1833	Ballyscullion	Philadelphia	RC
DOHERTY, Michael	24	1833	Ballyscullion	Philadelphia	RC
McLAUGHLIN, Catherine	20	1833	Ballycarton	Quebec	RC
McCORMICK, Patrick	25	1833	Duncrun	Philadelphia	RC
McCormick, William	23	1833	Duncrun	Philadelphia	RC
KENEDY, James	20	1834	Duncrun	New York	RC
DOHERTY, John	22	1834	Duncrun	Quebec	RC
RUDDEN, William	24	1833	Ballycarton	Quebec	RC
McLAUGHLIN, Catherine	26	1833	Ballycarton	Quebec	RC
KILMARY, Abraham	30	1834	Ballycarton	Quebec	RC
KANE, Hugh	23	1833	Claggan	Philadelphia	RC
SMITH, Robert	23	1833	Ballyscullion	Philadelphia	RC
McLAUGHLIN, Mark	30	1833	Ballyleighery	Quebec	RC
FERSON, William	24	1833	Ballymultimber	Philadelphia	P
DOHERTY, William	24	1833	Ballymultimber	Philadelphia	P
SNELL, Mary Ann	28	1834	Servant at Bellerena	Quebec	EC
TATE, Samuel	28	1833	Woodtown	Quebec	P
TATE, Thomas	20	1833	Woodtown	Quebec	P
PATERSON, Thomas	35	1833	Woodtown	Quebec	EC
McNALLY, James	30	1833	Aughill	Quebec	RC
McNALLY, Margaret	21	1833	Aughill	Quebec	RC
REDGATE, George	25	1833	Aughill	New York	RC
McFEELY, William	24	1834	Aughill	New York	RC
FARREN, James	25	1833	Aughill	Quebec	RC
DOHERTY, Ellen	20	1833	Tircreveen	Quebec	RC
GILCHRIST, William	40	1834	Ballymaclary	Quebec	RC
GILCHRIST, Sarah	41	1834	Ballymaclary	Quebec	RC
GILCHRIST, John	10	1834	Ballymaclary	Quebec	RC
GILCHRIST, William Jun	8	1834	Ballymaclary	Quebec	RC
GILCHRIST, Catherine	12	1834	Ballymaclary	Quebec	RC
O'BRIEN, Holland	25	1834	Ballymaclary	Quebec	RC
O'BRIEN, Margaret	35	1834	Ballymaclary	Quebec	RC
TONNER, Margaret	7	1834	Ballymaclary	Quebec	RC
McCAGUE, Margaret	24	1834	Clooney	Quebec	RC
O'KANE, Ellen	20	1833	Clooney	St John	RC
O'KANE, Margaret	18	1833	Clooney	St John	RC
McCAGUE, Nancy	22	1833	Clooney	St John	RC
DOHERTY, George	26	1834	Upper Drummanus	New York	RC
DOHERTY, Nancy	22	1833	Upper Drummanus	Philadelphia	RC
McTYRE, Hugh	22	1833	Upper Drummanus	Quebec	RC
McTYRE, Betty	25	1833	Upper Drummanus	Quebec	RC
SMITH, Robert	24	1833	Upper Drummanus	Philadelphia	RC

ORDNANCE SURVEY MEMOIRS

COUNTY: LONDONDERRY

PARISH: TAMLAGHT FINLAGAN

NAME	AGE	YEAR LEFT	TOWNLAND	DESTINATION	RELI-GION
McCLANE, Sally Jane	22	1834	Ballymore	New York	P
WARK, David	20	1834	Ballymore	New York	P
BAIRD, James	58	1833	Ballymore	Philadelphia	p
BAIRD, William	28	1833	Ballymore	Philadelphia	P
BAIRD, James Jun	23	1833	Ballymore	Philadelphia	P
BAIRD, Robert	18	1833	Ballymore	Philadelphia	P
BAIRD, John	9	1833	Ballymore	Philadelphia	P
BAIRD, Ann	30	1833	Ballymore	Philadelphia	P
BAIRD, Elenor	27	1833	Ballymore	Philadelphia	P
BAIRD, Maryann	14	1833	Ballymore	Philadelphia	P
BAIRD, Martha	7	1833	Ballymore	Philadelphia	P
McCANLIS, John	25	1833	Ballymore	Philadelphia	P
STEWART, John	40	1834	Ballymore	Philadelphia	P
STEWART, Jane	40	1834	Ballymore	Philadelphia	P
STEWART, William	16	1834	Ballymore	Philadelphia	P
STEWART, John	14	1834	Ballymore	Philadelphia	P
STEWART, Robert	12	1834	Ballymore	Philadelphia	P
STEWART, Hugh	1	1834	Ballymore	Philadelphia	P
STEWART, Jane	10	1834	Ballymore	Philadelphia	P
STEWART, Elizabeth	8	1834	Ballymore	Philadelphia	P
STEWART, Maryann	6	1834	Balllymore	Philadelphia	P
MORRISON, Andrew	22	1834	Moys	Philadelphia	P
McCRACKEN, Joseph	20	1834	Moys	Quebec	P
NEILEY, James	25	1833	Moys	Quebec	P
NEILEY, Joseph	23	1833	Moys	Philadelphia	P
PURSLEY, Robert	24	1833	Ballynarrig	Philadelphia	P
PURSLEY, Robert	52	1834	Ballynarrig	New York	P
PURSLEY, Elizabeth	50	1834	Ballynarrig	New York	P
PURSLEY, Ann	18	1834	Ballynarrig	New York	P
PURSLEY, Rachel	16	1834	Ballynarrig	New York	P
PURSLEY, David	12	1834	Ballynarrig	New York	P
NEILEY, William	50	1833	Ballynarrig	Philadelphia	P
NEILEY, Jane	40	1833	Ballynarrig	Philadelphia	P
NEILEY, James	20	1833	Ballynarrig	Philadelphia	P
NEILEY, William	15	1833	Ballynarrig	Philadelphia	P
NEILEY, John	25	1833	Ballynarrig	Philadelphia	P
NEILEY, Maryann	22	1833	Ballynarrig	Philadelphia	P
ALCORN, Andrew	20	1834	Ballynarrig	Philadelphia	P
ALCORN, Martha	20	1834	Ballynarrig	Philadelphia	P
GETTY, Joseph	20	1834	Ballynarrig	Philadelphia	P
McCOOK, John	60	1833	Largy	Philadelphia	P
McCOOK, Jane	56	1833	Largy	Philadelphia	P
McCOOK, William	30	1833	Largy	Philadelphia	P
McCOOK, Joseph	24	1833	Largy	Philadelphia	P
McCOOK, Hugh	22	1833	Largy	Philadelphia	P
NEILEY, Eacy	20	1833	Largy	Philadelphia	P
BEER, James	22	1834	Largy	PHiladelphia	P
BEER, Samuel	26	1834	Largy	Philadelphia	P
BEER, Elizabeth	24	1833	Largy	Philadelphia	P
BEER, Jane	20	1834	Largy	Philadelphia	P
JACKSON, Margret	20	1833	Largy	Philadelphia	P
CAMPBELL, John	46	1834	Magheramore	St John	P
CAMPBELL, Mary	44	1834	Magheramore	St John	P
CAMPBELL, Maryann	9	1834	Magheramore	St John	P
GILDERSON, William	40	1834	Magheramore	St John	RC
GILDERSON, Ann	40	1834	Magheramore	St John	RC
GILDERSON, Thomas	8	1834	Magheramore	St John	RC
GILDERSON, William	4	1834	Magheramore	St John	RC
GILDERSON, John	2	1834	Magheramore	St John	RC
GILDERSON, Mary	6	1834	Magheramore	St John	RC
LOWRY, John	32	1834	Magheramore	Philadelphia	P
LOWRY, Mary	30	1833	Largy	Philadelphia	P
MULLEN, James	40	1834	Drumreghlin	Philadelphia	RC
MULLEN, Sarah	40	1834	Drumreghlin	Philadelphia	RC

97

COUNTY: LONDONDERRY

PARISH: TAMLAGHT FINLAGAN

NAME	AGE	YEAR LEFT	TOWNLAND	DESTINATION	RELI-GION
MULLEN, Ann	10	1834	Drumreghlin	Philadelphia	RC
MULLEN, Margaret	8	1834	Drumreghlin	Philadelphia	RC
MULLEN, Jane	6	1834	Drumreghlin	Philadelphia	RC
MULLEN, Sally	4	1834	Drumreghlin	Philadelphia	RC
McDONNALD, James	35	1834	Drumreghlin	Quebec	P
McDONNALD, Andrew	30	1834	Drumreghlin	Quebec	P
McDONNALD, William	24	1834	Drumreghlin	Quebec	P
McDONNALD, Eliza	32	1834	Drumreghlin	Quebec	P
McLAUGHLIN, Edward	24	1834	Drumreghlin	St John	RC
PICKET, William	19	1834	Tamlaght	New York	EC
PICKET, Mary	16	1834	Tamlaght	New York	EC
KERR, John	22	1834	Tamlaght	Philadelphia	P
McCOOK, James	22	1833	Tamlaght	Philadelphia	P
McCOOK, John	20	1834	Tamlaght	Philadelphia	P
HUTCHINSON, John	20	1833	Tamlaght	New York	P
HUTCHINSON, James	23	1833	Tamlaght	New York	P
McCAY, Patrick	30	1833	Tamlaght	New York	RC
THOMPSON, John	30	1834	Drumacarney	New York	P
THOMPSON, Henery	26	1834	Drumacarney	New York	P
HUNTER, Scott	26	1833	Tartnakelly	Philadelphia	P
CARTIN, Maryann	26	1834	Tartnakelly	Philadelphia	P
CARTIN, Michael	28	1834	Tartnakelly	Philadelphia	RC
O'KANE, John	26	1834	Tartnakelly	St John	RC
MORRISON, Thomas White	20	1834	Dromore	Philadelphia	P
MORRISON, John White	18	1834	Dromore	Philadelphia	P
STEWART, John	24	1834	Dromore	Philadelphia	P
CASKEY, Samuel	50	1834	Dromore	Philadelphia	P
CASKEY, Ann	47	1834	Dromore	Philadelphia	P
CASKEY, John	22	1833	Dromore	Philadelphia	P
CASKEY, Mary	24	1834	Dromore	Philadelphia	P
CASKEY, Eliza	22	1834	Dromore	Philadelphia	P
CASKEY, Ann	20	1834	Dromore	Philadelphia	P
CASKEY, Milly	18	1834	Dromore	Philadelphia	P
CASKEY, Margret Jane	16	1834	Dromore	Philadelphia	P
CRAFORD, Joseph	26	1833	Culmore	Philadelphia	P
WILSON, John	20	1834	Clagan	Philadelphia	P
DEVINE, John	30	1834	Glack	Philadelphia	RC
CRAIG, John	20	1833	Sistrakeel	Philadelphia	RC
CRAIG, Magy	18	1833	Sistrakeel	Philadelphia	RC
McCAULEY, Robert	30	1834	Glasveagh	St John	P
GORDON, George	18	1834	Glasveagh	St John	P
HEALEY, Neil	28	1833	Ballyking	St John	P
HEALEY, Margret	26	1833	Ballyking	St John	RC
HEALEY, Maryann	4	1833	Ballyking	St John	RC
HEALEY, Eliza	2	1833	Ballyking	St John	RC
HEALEY, John	50 Days	1833	Ballyking	St John	RC
WHITE, John	19	1834	Ballyking	St John	P
McCAULEY, James	30	1833	Ballyking	St John	P
McCAULEY, Ann	28	1833	Ballyking	St John	P
McCAULEY, (Girl)	4	1833	Ballyking	St John	P
McCAULEY, (Girl)	2	1833	Ballyking	St John	P
McENTIRE, Margret	18	1834	Drummond	St John	P
LITTLEWOOD, Ann	24	1834	Drummond	St John	RC
STEWART, Christopher	24	1834	Ballykelly	New York	EC
CAMPBELL, James	28	1834	Ballykelly	New York	P
DIAMOND, John	28	1834	Ballykelly	New York	P
DIAMOND, Daniel	26	1834	Ballykelly	New York	P
IRVINE, Thomas	22	1833	Ballykelly	Quebec	P
CONNOR, Matilda	22	1833	Ballykelly	St John	EC
DEARMOTT, Andrew	40	1834	Ballykelly	Quebec	P
DEARMOTT, Ann	25	1834	Ballykelly	Quebec	P
DEARMOTT, Eliza	9	1834	Ballykelly	Quebec	P
DEARMOTT, Sallyann	7	1834	Ballykelly	Quebec	P
DEARMOTT, Fanney	3	1834	Ballykelly	Quebec	P

COUNTY: LONDONDERRY
PARISH: TAMLAGHT FINLAGAN

NAME	AGE	YEAR LEFT	TOWNLAND	DESTINATION	RELI-GION
DEARMOTT, (Girl)	1	1834	Ballykelly	Quebec	P
McCLOSKEY, Owen	30	1834	Ballykelly	Quebec	RC
McCLOSKEY, Patrick	28	1834	Ballykelly	Quebec	RC
McLAUGHLIN, John	50	1834	Ballykelly	St John	P
McLAUGHLIN, Ann	50	1834	Ballykelly	St John	P
McLAUGHLIN, Martha	22	1834	Ballykelly	St John	P
McLAUGHLIN, Catherine	24	1834	Ballykelly	St John	P
McGAUY, Ann	50	1834	Ballykelly	St John	RC
McGAUY, Maria	20	1834	Ballykelly	St John	RC
McGAUY, Ann	8	1834	Ballykelly	St John	RC
McGEE, Margret	45	1834	Ballykelly	St John	EC
McGEE, Matty	32	1834	Ballykelly	St John	EC
McGEE, Eliza	1	1834	Ballykelly	St John	EC
IRVINE, Ann	18	1834	Walworth	St John	P
MILLER, Margret	18	1834	Finlagan	St John	EC
LATTEN, John	20	1833	Drumbally Donaghey	New York	P
MITCHEL, Solomon	35	1833	Drumbally Donaghey	New York	RC
MITCHEL, Susanna	36	1833	Drumbally Donaghey	New York	RC
MITCHEL, Thomas	12	1833	Drumbally Donaghey	New York	RC
MITCHEL, John	10	1833	Drumbally Donaghey	New York	RC
MITCHEL, Joseph	8	1833	Drumbally Donaghey	New York	RC
MITCHEL, Maryann	6	1833	Drumbally Donaghey	New York	RC
MITCHEL, Rosey	4	1833	Drumbally Donaghey	New York	RC
MITCHEL, Susanna	2	1833	Drumbally Donaghey	New York	RC
MARTIN, Daniel	22	1834	Ardmargle	Philadelphia	P
PIPER, William	22	1833	Corndale	Philadelphia	P
LAGAN, William	22	1833	Burnally	Philadelphia	P
O'KANE, Mary	24	1834	Lomond	Quebec	RC
O'KANE, William	20	1833	Lomond	Quebec	RC
STEWART, Thomas	50	1833	Lomond	Quebec	P
STEWART, James	46	1833	Lomond	Quebec	P
STEWART, John	22	1833	Lomond	Quebec	P
STEWART, James	17	1833	Lomond	Quebec	P
STEWART, Thomas	15	1833	Lomond	Quebec	P
STEWART, Alexander	13	1833	Lomond	Quebec	P
STEWART, Barton	11	1833	Lomond	Quebec	P
STEWART, Jane	9	1833	Lomond	Quebec	P
STEWART, Rachael	2	1833	Lomond	Quebec	P
IRVIN, Robert	20	1833	Culmore	Quebec	P
PEERY, Alexander	22	1833	Culmore	New York	P
PEERY, Maryann	18	1833	Culmore	New York	P
SMITH, Ann	50	1833	Ballyhendry	Philadelphia	P
SMITH, John	24	1833	Ballyhendry	Philadelphia	P
SMITH, Eliza	18	1833	Ballyhendry	Philadelphia	P
CROTHERS, Samuel	24	1833	Carramuddle	Philadelphia	P
CROTHERS, Margret	20	1832	Carramuddle	Philadelphia	P
CROTHERS, Eliza	3	1833	Carramuddle	Philadelphia	P
CROTHERS, Jane	6	1833	Carramuddle	Philadelphia	P
CROTHERS, Maryann	1	1833	Carramuddle	Philadelphia	P
KING, William	60	1833	Carramuddle	New York	P
KING, John	40	1833	Carramuddle	New York	P
KING, James	38	1833	Carramuddle	New York	P
KING, William	20	1833	Carramuddle	New York	P
KING, Jane	34	1833	Carramuddle	New York	P
MILLER, Joseph	25	1833	Carramuddle	New York	P
MILLER, Catherine	24	1833	Carramuddle	New York	P
MILLER, Elenor	2	1833	Carramuddle	New York	P
GAULT, William	18	1834	Muirglasgow	New York	EC
McLAUGHLIN, Robert	24	1833	Muirglasgow	New York	EC
SLOAN, William	20	1833	Muirglasgow	Philadelphia	P
SLOAN, David	24	1833	Muirglasgow	Philadelphia	P
WARK, William	18	1833	Broheris	New York	P
WARK, Mary Jane	20	1833	Broheris	New York	P
TORRENS, Mary	26	1834	Carrareagh	New York	P

ORDNANCE SURVEY MEMOIRS

COUNTY: LONDONDERRY
PARISH: TAMLAGHT FINLAGAN

NAME	AGE	YEAR LEFT	TOWNLAND	DESTINATION	RELI-GION
McLAUGHLIN, Margaret	20	1834	Carraclare	New York	P
WARK, Samuel	20	1834	Farlow	New York	P
WARK, Jacob	18	1833	Farlow	New York	P
SIMPSON, John	24	1833	Farlow	New York	P
SIMPSON, Eliza	22	1833	Farlow	New York	P
DOGHERTY, William	30	1834	Farlow	New York	RC
DOGHERTY, Margaret	28	1834	Farlow	New York	RC
DOGHERTY, Robert	5	1834	Farlow	New York	RC
DOGHERTY, John	7	1834	Farlow	New York	RC
DOGHERTY, Sally	3	1834	Farlow	New York	RC
DOGHERTY, Ann	1	1834	Farlow	New York	RC
MOORE, John	28	1833	Money Rannel	Quebec	P
IRVINE, Margret	26	1833	Money Rannel	Quebec	P
IRVINE, Maryann	20	1833	Money Rannel	Quebec	P
WHITE, Joseph	22	1833	Shanreagh	Quebec	P
JOHNSTON, John	22	1833	Shanreagh	Quebec	RC
JOHNSTON, Mrs	20	1833	Shanreagh	Quebec	RC

COUNTY: LONDONDERRY
PARISH: TAMLAGHT O'CRILLY

NAME	AGE	YEAR LEFT	TOWNLAND	DESTINATION	RELI-GION
QUIN, John	22	1834	Bovedy	New York	P
GILMORE, Margret	20	1834	Bovedy	New York	P
GILMORE, Alexander	22	1834	Bovedy	New York	P
STARRITT, John	30	1834	Killygullib	Quebec	P
McCONNELL, John	26	1834	Killygullib	Quebec	RC
McCONNELL, James	22	1834	Killygullib	Quebec	RC
McPEAKE, Margret	30	1834	Killygullib	Quebec	RC
MALOY, Rose	26	1834	Ballynian	Quebec	RC
DIMOND, James	26	1834	Killymuck	New York	RC
CAMPBELL, Robert	24	1834	Lisnagroat	St John	P
CAMPBELL, John	25	1834	Drumnacanon	St John	P
CAMPBELL, Ann	29½	1834	Drumnacanon	St John	P
WORKMAN, Sarah	24	1834	Drumnacanon	St John	P
WORKMAN, Ann	21	1834	Drumnacanon	St John	P
TOLE, Henry	24	1834	Inishrush	New York	RC
TOLE, Mary	24	1834	Inishrush	New York	RC
TOLE, John	1	1834	Inishrush	New York	RC
HILTON, Robert	40	1834	Ballymacpeake	New York	P
HILTON, William	18	1834	Ballymacpeake	New York	P
HILTON, John	16	1834	Ballymacpeake	New York	P
WORKMAN, Hugh	40	1834	Drumoolish	New York	P
WORKMAN, Eliza	60	1834	Drumoolish	New York	P
WORKMAN, Paul	35	1834	Drumoolish	New York	P
WORKMAN, Mary	22	1834	Drumoolish	New York	P
WORKMAN, Robert	20	1834	Drumoolish	New York	P
WORKMAN, Margret	1	1834	Drumoolish	New York	P
NEILL, Thomas	20	1834	Drumoolish	New York	P
MILLER, William	25	1834	Glenone	New York	EC
MILLER, Ann	33	1834	Glenone	New York	EC
RAINEY, Robert	22	1834	Glenone	New York	RC
RAINEY, Catherine	20	1834	Glenone	New York	RC
HENERY, Henry	21	1834	Glenone	New York	RC
SCULLION, Henry	20	1834	Glenone	New York	RC
McMULLAN, Ann	19	1834	Glenone	New York	RC
KANE, James	20	1834	Glenone	New York	RC
McLAUGHLIN, William	23	1834	Tyanee	New York	P
MADIGAN, John	26	1834	Tyanee	New York	RC
QUIN, John	30	1835	Bovedy	St John	RC
QUIN, Mary	25	1835	Bovedy	St John	RC
QUIN, Bridget	3	1835	Bovedy	St John	RC
QUIN, Mary Jane	1½	1835	Bovedy	St John	RC
McCONNELL, Patrick	24	1835	Killygullib	Quebec	RC
QUIN, John	30	1835	Killygullib	Quebec	RC
QUIN, Mary	28	1835	Killygullib	Quebec	RC
QUIN, Bridget	2	1835	Killygullib	Quebec	RC
QUIN, Mary	½	1835	Killygullib	Quebec	RC
BRADLEY, Patrick	18	1835	Drumagarner	Quebec	RC
CRILLY, Mary	27	1835	Ballynian	Quebec	RC
CRILLY, Catherine	20	1835	Ballynian	Quebec	RC
DUNCAN, Robert	26	1835	Lismoyle	New York	P
DUNCAN, Mary	28	1835	Lismoyle	New York	P
STEWART, James	30	1835	Killymuck	Quebec	P
STEWART, Charlot	26	1835	Killymuck	Quebec	P
STEWART, John	6	1835	Killymuck	Quebec	P
STEWART, Sarah	4	1835	Killymuck	Quebec	P
STEWART, Mary	2	1835	Killymuck	Quebec	P
McCOLLIAN, William	30	1835	Drumsaragh	St John	P
McCOLLIAN, Eliza	26	1835	Drumsaragh	St John	P
McCOLLIAN, John	3	1835	Drumsaragh	St John	P
GRAHAM, Andrew	30	1835	Drumsaragh	St John	P
DOUGLAS, William	22	1835	Drumsaragh	St John	P
DOUGLAS, Margaret	25	1835	Drumsaragh	St John	P
GRAHAM, Eliza	28	1835	Drumsaragh	St John	P
JOHNSTONE, Ritchard	38	1835	Drumane	St John	P

COUNTY: LONDONDERRY

PARISH: TAMLAGHT O'CRILLY

NAME	AGE	YEAR LEFT	TOWNLAND	DESTINATION	RELI-GION
JOHNSTONE, Eliza	36	1835	Drumane	St John	P
JOHNSTONE, James	8	1835	Drumane	St John	P
JOHNSTONE, Henry	6	1835	Drumane	St John	P
JOHNSTONE, Jane	4	1835	Drumane	St John	P
JOHNSTONE, Ritchard	2	1835	Drumane	St John	P
MOONEY, Henery	65	1835	Drumane	St John	EC
MOONEY, Mary	75	1835	Drumane	St John	EC
KIRKWOOD, John	21	1835	Moneysallin	St John	P
McCLOY, William	20	1835	Ballymacpeake	St John	P
CAMPBELL, William	24	1835	Drumard	St John	P
BOLTON, Eliza	20	1835	Drumard	New York	P
McLACY, Patrick	23	1835	Killygullib	Quebec	RC
McCANN, James	20	1835	Drumagarner	Quebec	RC

COUNTY: LONDONDERRY
PARISH: TERMONEENY

NAME	AGE	YEAR LEFT	TOWNLAND	DESTINATION	RELI-GION
MACKRELL, Thomas	18	1834	Ballynahone More	Philadelphia	I
MACKRELL, Esther	20	1834	Ballynahone More	Philadelphia	I
ATKINSON, John	28	1834	Ballynahone More	Philadelphia	P
ATKINSON, Sarah	32	1834	Ballynahone More	Philadelphia	P
McDONALD, William	30	1834	Ballynahone More	Quebec	P
McDONALD, Isabella	25	1834	Ballynahone More	Quebec	P
RICHARDSON, Hugh	30	1834	Ballynahone More	Quebec	P
RICHARDSON, Anne	34	1834	Ballynahone More	Quebec	P
HENRY, Arthur	16	1834	Carricknakeilt	Philadelphia	P
TAYLOR, William	35	1834	Carricknakeilt	Philadelphia	P
TAYLOR, William Jun	30	1834	Carricknakeilt	Philadelphia	P
TAYLOR, Andrew	40	1834	Carricknakeilt	Philadelphia	P
TAYLOR, Robert	45	1834	Carricknakeilt	Philadelphia	P
NEEVIN, Lawson	22	1834	Carricknakeilt	Philadelphia	P
MONTGOMERY, James	30	1834	Carricknakeilt	Phiadelphia	P
ORRELL, Robert	36	1834	Cabragh	New York	P
SCULLION, Hugh	22	1834	Broagh	New York	P
SCULLION, Margaret	18	1834	Broagh	New York	P
McDONALD, Mary	30	1834	Broagh	Philadelphia	P
KERR, James	35	1834	Broagh	New York	P
GREGG, Hugh	50	1834	Derganagh	Quebec	I
GREGG, Eliza	25	1834	Derganagh	Quebec	I
HOOD, James	32	1834	Derganagh	Quebec	P
KERR, James	40	1834	Derganagh	Quebec	P
GREGG, John	20	1834	Derganagh	Quebec	I
GREGG, Ellen	18	1834	Derganagh	Quebec	I
GREGG, Joseph	16	1834	Derganagh	Quebec	I
GREGG, Anne Jane	14	1834	Derganagh	Quebec	I
GREGG, David	12	1834	Derganagh	Quebec	I
GREGG, Maryanne	10	1834	Derganagh	Quebec	I
GREGG, Hugh) Twins	8	1834	Derganagh	Quebec	I
GREGG, David)	8	1834	Derganagh	Quebec	I
PAUL, Anne Jane	22	1834	Mullagh	Quebec	P
PAUL, Mary	20	1834	Mullagh	Quebec	P
PAUL, Andrew	24	1834	Mullagh	Quebec (Returned)	P
SAVAGE, Robert	27	1835	Carricknakeilt	New York	P
AGNESS, John	40	1835	Broagh	New York	P
MAGUCIAN, Clotworthy	40	1835	Broagh	New York	RC
MAGUCIAN, Margaret	19	1835	Broagh	New York	RC
KILGORE, James	46	1835	Ballynahone	Quebec	I
KILGORE, Martha	35	1835	Ballynahone	Quebec	I
BEAR, Thomas	30	1835	Lurgangoose	Quebec	I
AVERILL, John	25	1835	Lurgangoose	Quebec	EC
AVERILL, Sarah	20	1835	Lurgangoose	Quebec	EC
AVERILL, David	1	1835	Lurgangoose	Quebec	EC
GIBSON, William	20	1835	Knocknakielt	Quebec	P
McCRACKIN, Alexander	30	1835	Knocknakielt	Quebec	P
McCRACKIN, David	27	1835	Knocknakielt	Quebec	P

COUNTY: LONDONDERRY
PARISH: TERMONEENY

NAME	AGE	YEAR LEFT	TOWNLAND	DESTINATION	RELI-GION
PEEBLES, John	30		Ballynahone More	Glasgow	P
HEPSON, John	22		Ballynahone More	Glasgow	EC
McDONALD, William	25		Ballynahone More	Glasgow	EC
CAMPBELL, James	20		Ballynahone More	Glasgow	EC
SHIELS, John	25		Ballynahone More	Glasgow	RC
SHIELS, Philip	30		Ballynahone More	Glasgow	RC
McCONAGHTY, Samuel	40		Ballynahone More	Glasgow	RC
O'NEIL, Cornelius	40		Ballynahone More	Glasgow	RC
DELAYAN, Bernard	25		Broagh	Glasgow	RC
McFALL, Charles	25		Broagh	Glasgow	RC
McFALL, John	18		Broagh	Glasgow	RC
McFALL, James	60		Broagh	Glasgow	RC
SCULLION, Daniel	25		Broagh	Glasgow	RC
KEENAN, Martha	28		Broagh	Glasgow	RC
SONAGH, John	46		Broagh	Glasgow	RC
SONAGH, Hugh	18		Broagh	Glasgow	RC
DONAHOE, Patrick	20		Broagh	Glasgow	RC
McPEAKE, Patrick	24		Broagh	Glasgow	RC
COSTELLO, James	60		Broagh	Glasgow	RC
COSTELLO, Michael	27		Broagh	Glasgow	RC
KANE, John	30		Broagh	Glasgow	RC
MAGUIRE, James	30		Broagh	Glasgow	RC
MAGUIRE, Frank	32		Broagh	Glasgow	RC
BRANAN, Rodger	55		Broagh	Glasgow	RC
BRANAN, John	22		Broagh	Glasgow	RC
BRANAN, James	18		Broagh	Glasgow	RC
McDONALD, John	20		Broagh	Glasgow	RC
CAMPBELL, Neil	20		Broagh	Glasgow	RC
McDONALD, Archibald	15		Broagh	Glasgow	RC
BRANAN, James	40		Broagh	Glasgow	RC
BRANAN, John	18		Broagh	Glasgow	RC
McILWEE, Charles	20		Broagh	Glasgow	RC
McILWEE, James	24		Broagh	Glasgow	RC
McILWEE, John	22		Broagh	Glasgow	RC
SCULLION, Bernard	18		Broagh	Glasgow	RC
SCULLION, John	23		Broagh	Glasgow	RC
COSTELLO, Patrick	20		Broagh	Glasgow	RC
BERRY, Theady	30		Broagh	Glasgow	RC
McILWEE, James	45		Broagh	Glasgow	RC
MULLIN, Daniel	17		Broagh	Glasgow	RC
McWILLIAMS, Hugh	30		Broagh	Glasgow	RC
McWILLIAMS, Frank	40		Broagh	Glasgow	RC
McCLARMAN, Patrick	35		Broagh	Glasgow	RC
McGURK, Michael	32		Broagh	Glasgow	RC
McGURK, James	25		Broagh	Glasgow	RC
McGURK, Patrick	27		Broagh	Glasgow	RC
McCONOMEY, Michael	30		Broagh	Glasgow	RC
BRANAN, James	26		Broagh	Glasgow	RC
SHEPHERD, James	20		Knocknakeilt	Glasgow	P
HEPSON, John	60		Derganagh	Glasgow	EC
AVERILL, Thomas	30		Lurgangoose	Glasgow	EC
MARTIN, Henry	30		Lurgangoose	Glasgow	EC
MARTIN, George	36		Lurgangoose	Glasgow	EC

114

WILLIAMSON, James, 73 , 94
  Jane, 54 , 54
  Margaret, 73
  Margaret Jun, 54
  Mary, 54
WILSON, Charles, 78
  Hannah, 89
  Hester, 71
  James, 5 , 83
  John, 6 , 12 , 21 , 98
  Joseph, 89
  ~Mary, 12 , 33 , 89
  Nancy, 21
  Robert, 13
  Thomas, 90
WINNON, John, 6
WINTON, Ellen, 90 , 91
  Jane, 90 , 90 , 91
  William, 90
WISELY, Margaret, 77
  Martin, 77
  William 77
WISEMAN, Anne, 5
  Archy, 3
WITHEROW, Samuel, 6
WOODS, John, 68
WOODSIDE, Alexander, 8
~WORKMAN, Ann, 101
  Eliza, 101
  Hugh, 101
  James, 6
  John, 41 , 57
  Margaret, 57 , 101
  Mary, 41 , 57 , 101
  Mary Jun, 41
  Paul, 101
  Richard, 57
  Robert, 101
  Sarah, 101
  William, 57
WRIGHT, Catherine, 30
  James, 30 , 72
  Joseph, 6 , 87
  Sarah, 80
YEATES, Mathew, 83
YOUNG, Henry, 32
  Hugh, 74
  John, 3
  Peter, 7
  William, 57

118